HERE'S WHAT PEOPLE A
CAROL McLEOD AND *TODAY IS A VERB…*

This new book by Carol McLeod provides biblical truth to questions we must all answer, like "What is my response for what has happened to me?" By encouraging believers to release control of our circumstances, we can fully put our *trust* in the One who knows it all already. He alone can safely lead us through. What a clarion message for today!

—*Johnie Hampton*
Founder and CEO, Hampton Creative

Carol McLeod delivers once again, bringing us a fresh perspective on living every day intentionally. As she so eloquently states, "Perhaps the answer lies in transforming *today* from a time period to an activity—from a noun to a verb." This book will challenge all of us to allow the Holy Spirit to change and encourage us to live boldly every day.

—*Donna M. Russo*
Festival director/CFO, Kingdom Bound Ministries

Today Is a Verb isn't just a book. It's a friend, warm and wise and pouring out. Birthed from six decades of living her story and loving Jesus, these practical, humble words disciple a generation of lost souls. One would be amiss to let Carol's new book get away. After all, one does not pass up on the chance to make a good friend.

—*Emily T. Wierenga*
Author, *God Who Became Bread*
President, The Lulu Tree Foundation

If you're looking for a hope-filled, celebratory devotional that makes your heart sing, then *Today Is a Verb* is for you. Carol McLeod, through recounting her own journey, holds the hand of every reader and gives them an opportunity to do everything from rejoice to persevere and overcome, all written in absolute love and encouragement. I'm smiling as I write this endorsement, as her words remind me to be in constant celebration of being His. This is a must read.

—*Angie Haskell*
Author, *Sugarcoated*

Carol McLeod offers substantive, thought-provoking daily devotionals that will urge you to action, as strong verbs should. *Today Is a Verb* guides readers through the process of applying biblical principles to daily living. Its interactive questions will help you stop, think, pray, and do the Lord's will while *"it is still called 'today'"* (Hebrews 3:13). Carol's personal narrative supports her solid scriptural teaching, which is enriched with quotes and daily declarations that will be revisited day after day. May God bless this new book for all who read it!

—*Amy Lively*
Author, speaker, and Bible teacher

Today Is a Verb by Carol McLeod is a game-changer for anyone tired of letting life just happen to them. This book is like a daily shot of espresso for the soul, waking you up to the power of intentional living. Carol's heartfelt guidance and practical tips turn mundane moments into extraordinary opportunities. Whether you're looking to rejoice, hope, or serve, each chapter in this thirty-day devotional is packed with wisdom and wit. Trust me, you'll laugh, you'll cry, and you might even dance a little. So, grab this book and start *today-ing* with gusto. Your future self will thank you!

—*Chris Busch*
President and CEO, LightQuest Media

I loved Carol McLeod's new book, *Today Is a Verb*. I will use this devotional time and again as a monthly deep dive into the things of God. The personal stories Carol shares will entice and enthrall you to meditate on the thought for the day. The life quotes are inspirational, and the daily declarations are powerful. Wow! Thank you, Carol, for encouraging and teaching us to focus on today; as Dietrich Bonhoeffer said, "In the whole of world history there is always only one really significant hour—the present. ... If you want to find eternity, you must serve the times."

—*Tim Cameron*
Best-selling author, *The Forty-Day Word Fast*

In *Today Is a Verb*, author Carol McLeod presents a refreshing perspective on daily living, turning the mundane into the extraordinary. With profound insight and gentle encouragement, this devotional guide invites readers to embrace each moment with intentionality and purpose. The central premise revolves around the concept of *today* not merely as a fleeting period of time but as an active engagement with life itself. By shifting our perception from *today* as a static noun to an energetic verb, Carol challenges readers to seize the opportunities inherent in every passing moment while underscoring the importance of partnering with Christ in shaping a life of significance.

What sets *Today Is a Verb* apart is its emphasis on finding joy and fulfillment in the midst of ordinary routines. Instead of waiting for grand moments or future achievements, this daily devotional empowers readers to cultivate gratitude and awareness in their daily experiences. In doing so, they learn to recognize the sacredness of each passing day and the potential for transformation it holds.

Today Is a Verb is a thought-provoking and uplifting read that transcends the boundaries of traditional devotionals. With its timeless wisdom and heartfelt encouragement, it empowers readers to embrace each day as an opportunity for growth, joy, and connection with Jesus Christ! Whether you're seeking spiritual nourishment or simply a renewed perspective on life, this book offers invaluable guidance for transforming *today* into a vibrant and fulfilling journey.

—*Julie Seals*
Hope Dealer

A breath of life-giving, fresh air! We all long for days full of color. We want joy and for all our marks to matter. *Today Is a Verb* infuses a renewed hope to make so much more out of each day that God has gifted us this side of eternity. Through her sincere stories, impassioned personal touches, and continuous biblical basis, Carol offers a bright shift in perspective to open our eyes wide to the beauty and sunshine available right now, today, regardless of our circumstances. The priceless, precious pages will uplift your everyday life with a refreshed posture of praise. Each time I sat down to read Carol's words, the lights in my heart turned on. And I can't wait for you to be blessed by her once again!

—*Keri Eichberger*
Author, *Win Over Worry*

If you're looking for a unique, fresh, uplifting way to put meaning and purpose in every day, read *Today Is a Verb*. Carol McLeod gives us thirty key words to contemplate, explore, understand, and intentionally live out *today*! This book is totally different from any devotional you've ever read—and you'll live out your faith with more joy and fulfillment as you put these biblical action words to work in your life.

—*Carol Kent*
Executive director, Speak Up Ministries
Author, *He Holds My Hand*

Have you ever thought about what it means to be a friend of God, not a slave? Friends are free to make choices; slaves are not. The blood of Jesus purchased your freedom. To enjoy this freedom means choosing every day to live proactively empowered by the Holy Spirit according to biblical action prompts. Carol McLeod's newest book, *Today Is a Verb*, is a perfect resource to help you identify powerful actions that are guaranteed to encourage a joy-filled victorious life. Purchasing this book provides more than principles. It will give you a coach, Carol McLeod, whose words on every page will encourage you to follow her example to exercise your freedom.

—*Faith Blatchford*
Author and creativity coach

Today Is A Verb is an inspiring book emphasizing the importance of seizing each day's opportunities and living with godly purpose and joy. Carol's message of embracing the possibilities and the greatness within us resonates with the idea of living life to its fullest potential. By aligning our actions with the Word of God, her book offers a guiding light in navigating the world's challenges and finding fulfillment in our spiritual journey. It is an uplifting valuable resource for anyone seeking motivation and guidance to lead a meaningful, fulfilled life.

—*Lee Ann Mancini*
Author, *Raising Kids to Follow Christ*

If you find yourself overwhelmed by worry and anxiety or fretting over events in the future that may or may not come to pass, you definitely need to pick up your copy of Carol's latest book *Today Is a Verb*. This work will help you press the emotional reset button to gain a fresh spiritual perspective. Carol invites you to shift your outlook and see your *today* not as a mere twenty-four-hour period, but as a dynamic opportunity to partner with God in living your life with intention, focusing on what matters most. When you choose to be fully present in each day, doing life with God at the helm, you'll say goodbye to strife, striving, and stress.

Carol does not leave you hanging on the how-to of it all. She distills biblical notions and those well-worn Scripture verses to a kind of practical energy fueled by the Holy Spirit inside you. Her messages speak right to your heart and mind with powerful words of encouragement to help you come fully alive each and every day! If you choose to live each day as a divine verb, your life will never be the same!

—*Victoria D. Lydon*, MA
Certified Christian Life Coach and podcaster

Psalm 90:12 reminds us to number our days, count them, make good use of them, and gain a heart of wisdom. Carol McLeod's new book *Today Is a Verb* will strengthen your resolve to not only make each day count, but to count each day as an opportunity for you to grow and become all God meant you to be. Today is your gift. Read *Today Is a Verb* and act on it with wisdom, enthusiasm, and joy. This book will show you how!

—*Karen Moore*
Devotional book author and speaker

Feeling like you're just watching your life pass you by? Take heart! Carol McLeod's *Today Is a Verb* is your wake-up call. This powerful book encourages you to stop being a passive observer and to begin actively participating in your own story and God's plan. Through wisdom, the Word, and practical guidance, McLeod motivates you to embrace God's purpose for your life, fill your days with meaning and intention, and radiate His light in the world around you. Ready to replace passive observation with purposeful action? Let *Today Is a Verb* ignite your passion and transform your life.

—*Laura Acuña*
Author, *Still Becoming: Hope, Help and Healing for the Diet-Weary Soul*

Life beckons us toward action, but for so many, our spirits are uncertain how to respond or how to move forward. *Today Is a Verb* offers relatable, encouraging, and rooted truth to bridge us from a status of *freeze and fear* to *free and fearless* instead by starting each day in God's abundant Word. Carol guides us on this journey with her timeless and life-giving encouragement in such a way that you truly feel a dear friend who genuinely cares for you is speaking. You will find that it speaks to the tender places in your own spirit to find healing, renewal, and tools to apply His holy Word. Find hope for your new *today* and inspiration to live life on purpose.

—*Cally Logan*
Author and speaker

TODAY *is a* VERB

Open the Gift of Now in Every Ordinary Moment

CAROL McLEOD

WHITAKER
HOUSE

TODAY IS A VERB

Open the Gift of Now in Every Ordinary Moment

carolmcleodministries.com
Carol McLeod Ministries | P.O. Box 1294 | Orchard Park, NY 14127

ISBN: 979-8-88769-278-4 | eBook ISBN: 979-8-88769-277-7
Printed in the United States of America
© 2024 by Carol McLeod

Whitaker House | 1030 Hunt Valley Circle | New Kensington, PA 15068
www.whitakerhouse.com

Library of Congress Cataloging-in-Publication Data
Names: McLeod, Carol Burton, 1954- author.
Title: Today is a verb : open the gift of now in every ordinary moment /
  Carol McLeod.
Description: New Kensington, PA : Whitaker House, [2024] | Summary:
  "Encourages readers to consider each day as a gift of time from God that
  can be lived to the fullest by purposely focusing on actions that can
  have practical and spiritual implications in their lives"— Provided by
  publisher.
Identifiers: LCCN 2024012284 (print) | LCCN 2024012285 (ebook) | ISBN
  9798887692784 | ISBN 9798887692777 (ebook)
Subjects: LCSH: Gifts—Religious aspects—Christianity. | Time—Religious
  aspects--Christianity. | God (Christianity) | Christian life. | BISAC:
  RELIGION / Christian Living / Women's Interests | BODY, MIND & SPIRIT /
  Inspiration & Personal Growth
Classification: LCC BR115.G54 M47 2024 (print) | LCC BR115.G54 (ebook) |
  DDC 234/.13—dc23/eng/20240516
LC record available at https://lccn.loc.gov/2024012284
LC ebook record available at https://lccn.loc.gov/2024012285

1 2 3 4 5 6 7 8 9 10 11 ⨆⨆ 31 30 29 28 27 26 25 24

DEDICATION

Enthusiastically dedicated to

Susie Hilchey—
My lifetime friend, sister, and cheerleader.
How I love *today-ing* with you!
I would rather *today* with you than anyone else!
Your heart ... your ever-present cheerfulness ...
and your commitment
to our friendship is a rare and priceless treasure.
Your love for Jesus is unmatched, and I am astounded watching
as you love and encourage others.
We were friends as young girls ... and now as seasoned women ...
the torch of friendship is still vibrant and warm.
Your life is a miracle ... it is a miracle of God's redemptive power
and His great faithfulness.

Thank you for teaching me how to *today*.

CONTENTS

FOREWORD

This year, my husband and I will celebrate our fortieth wedding anniversary. I love him more now than the day I said *yes* to him. I love God more now than I did back then too. We entered marriage with a sincere faith, wide eyes, and clueless hearts. We had no idea what we were about to face: My father's battle with cancer, high-risk pregnancies resulting in months of bedrest, babies in the hospital, contracting Lyme disease during one of my pregnancies, and my husband's battle with cancer.

In those early years, we didn't know what hit us. But we searched for God in the whirlwind of our trials and found Him in the eye of the storm. He taught us to look for the blessings in our battles. He taught us that being a believer is far more than embracing a proper theology that ensures passage to heaven. Being a follower of Christ means that we shift every aspect of who we are, all our lives, onto the promises of God. When we did that, things started to change. God's promises proved sturdier than our circumstances. We learned that the enemy doesn't have an endless supply of strength. And our trials trained us to walk triumphantly through every hardship.

One of the greatest blessings from those early years was this: on a much deeper level, we learned not to assume we were guaranteed many years of life. We learned to treasure the moments God entrusted to us. Being young parents and battling the diseases we did brought fresh revelation to this passage:

> *Teach us to number our days, that we may present to You a heart of wisdom.* —Psalm 90:12

None of us knows the extent of our days. We don't know how many tomorrows God has planned for us. *But we have today.* And today is a priceless, treasured gift from the One who knows your name. He's the One who put the stars in place. And the One who parts the seas, moves mountains, heals bodies, and brings prodigals home. We lose the impact of our days when we rush from one task to the next, fully forgetting how connected we are to heaven. But when we slow down and engage with God in our everyday moments? Everything changes.

To number your days is to appoint your days, anoint your days, and claim your days for the kingdom. It's to live with eternity in mind. Every hardship and every blessing in your life bursts with eternal possibilities. You're more spiritual than physical. If you are in Christ Jesus, the Spirit of the living God is alive in you! He's your down payment of the inheritance to come. He's your guard, guide, comfort, and correction. You're never alone. And He wants to add power to your steps, your words, your prayers, and your offerings.

If you long to break free from past regrets and cast your future cares on the Lord so you can be fully present in *this moment*, this book is for you. *Today Is a Verb* reminds us of the intimate access to the Most High. Carol McLeod writes:

> We serve a heavenly Father who is an extravagant and intentional gift-giver. He gives gifts on purpose and has not ignored one of us when it comes to the giving of extraordinary gifts.

What if you walked more intimately with God today? What if you approached today with more purposeful intentionality and holy expectancy? What if you invited Jesus into the center of your cares and concerns and trusted Him to do the impossible in your story? What if you fully shifted your weight onto the promises of God and began to trust Him with all that's happening in you and around you?

I'll tell you what will happen.

You'd see God's kingdom come to earth. He wants to do life with you. He wants to partner with you to transform your days in a way that changes the world. I dare you to trust Him.

God bless you as you read.

—Susie Larson
Bestselling author, national speaker, and talk radio host

ACKNOWLEDGMENTS

I was a cheerleader in high school, and I have never regretted it. There is just something deep within me that longs to vocalize my praise and admiration for those who are playing their hearts out.

I have an entire team of friends, family members, and ministry partners who are on the court of life and who are focused on the intrinsic joy of the game. These irreplaceable comrades are *today-ing* their way through life and have taught me how to live well, how to love well, and how to cheer enthusiastically.

Thank you, Craig, for choosing me, for serving the Lord wholeheartedly, and for so much kindness that I have never felt I deserved. Thank you for being a shepherd, a coach, and now a friend to our children. I am deeply grateful for you.

Thank you, Matthew, for forgiving me for all my first-time mama mistakes and for loving me still. Your strength, wisdom, and excellence never cease to amaze me. You are my son and my friend. You are always in my heart. I am profoundly thankful for you. Thank you for bringing Emily into our family and into our hearts. You were too brave, Emily, to enter this family filled with opinions, creativity, and strong wills! You have been a delight to us all, and I am grateful that you are my daughter-in-love. Olivia, Wesley, Boyce, and Elizabeth Joy are among the greatest gifts of my life.

Thank you, Christopher, for the gift of song that you have always provided for our family. You are truly the kindest person that I know. Whether you live near or far, you are always in my heart. I am infinitely grateful for you. Amelia and Jack are my delight! What extraordinary kids you are raising!

Thank you, Jordan, for your prayers, for your support, and for your cheerfulness. I don't just love you … but I also like you! You are our miracle child, and you were born to serve God at this moment in history. Live for Him always. You are always in my heart. Thank you, Allie, for choosing Jordan and for loving us all unconditionally. Your prayers have already moved mountains, and your heart for worship is pure and brave. Know that I am beyond grateful to call you my daughter-in-love and my friend! You will never know how much I love Ian and Isla; they are pure delight to this Marmee's heart.

Thank you, Joy, for always living up to your name and for lavishing the delight that is uniquely yours on everyone that you meet. You are my daughter and my friend. I am so proud of you, especially now. Your call to ministry and to motherhood is obvious. I am honored to be your mom. Haven Elizabeth has wrapped her little heart around my heart. I will always be grateful that I was chosen to be her Marmee.

Thank you, Joni, for the years of sweet camaraderie that we shared as you were growing up. Those were some of the very favorite days of my entire life. Know that I am your mom—and nothing will ever change that! You are loved completely. You are always in my heart. I am so thankful for you. Rozy and Luca Jo are gifts to our family, and I will love them forever.

Thank you, Mom and Leo, for your prayers, your faith, and your encouragement. I ache to be with you, but I know that the Lord is faithful in His care of you. I will always be *your girl*.

Thank you, Nanny, for your example of godly living and persistent prayer!

Thank you to my dad, Norman Burton, who has escaped time and now lives in eternity. I wouldn't be the woman I am today without your leadership and example. All the credit goes to you and all the glory goes to God!

Thank you to my dear friend and coworker, Angela Storm. You are a gift to me and to this ministry. Thank you for your labor of love, for your attention to details, for your prayer support, and for your faith. I love serving God with you!

Thank you to my friend and fellow warrior, Christy Christopher. You are making a difference, Christy. Never doubt the assignment on your life or the power that you have been given! I love *making hell smaller and heaven bigger* with you!

Thank you to Keri Spring, whose dedicated service to Carol McLeod Ministries has helped us to soar. You, my friend, are simply amazing! What did we ever do without Keri?!

Thank you to the entire staff of Carol McLeod Ministries: Angela Storm, Susan Meyers, Keri Spring, Kim Worden, and Christy Christopher. It is an undeserved honor to work with all of you as we endeavor to take the joy of His presence to this generation. You are appreciated, loved, and prayed for daily.

I must give a deep and sincere thank-you to the Carol McLeod Ministries Board of Directors: Angela Storm, Kim Pickard Dudley, Sue Hilchey, Shannon Maitre, Tim Harner, Taci Darnelle, Jenna Goldsmith, Rhae Buckley, and Suzanne Kuhn. All of you are the foundation of everything that we do. Thanks for being rock solid! Your wisdom, expertise, and personal support are invaluable.

It is my deep honor to give a rich and heartfelt thank-you to the entire staff at Whitaker House Publishers. You are simply the best in the business, and there is no one I would rather publish with than all of you. A sincere and loud *shout out* to Christine Whitaker, Amy Bartlett, Peg Fallon, and Becky Speer for your prayers, your heart for excellence, and your belief in this book.

Warrior Moms—What an honor it has been to fight battles with you! We are standing in strong faith that with God nothing is impossible. Thank you for holding up my arms in the battle.

Thank you also to the group of women who answer the desperate emails that come into Carol McLeod Ministries: Debby Summers, Diane Phelps, Shannon Maitre, Susie Hilchey, Beth Nash, Debby Edwards, Suzanne Adorian, Brenda Mutton, Laurie Rudolph, Elaine

Wheatley, Joanne Crain, Bridget Fenley, Joan Stevens, Kandus Patterson, Kim King, Linda Butz, Michelle Worden, Paula Sterns, Veda King, and Christy Christopher. God is using you in mighty and dramatic ways! I am honored to partner with you in prayer and in encouragement.

And then, to a magnificent team of friends who fill my life with encouragement and enthusiasm. Each one of you has taught me to live a life overflowing with hope and joy: Carolyn Hogan, Lisa Keller, Jill Dougherty, Bridget Fenley, Dawn Frink, Debby Edwards, Diane Phelps, Brenda Mutton, Elaine Wheatley, Marilynda Lynch, Joy Knox, Sue Hilchey, Kim Pickard Dudley, and Shannon Maitre.

And to Jesus, my Lord and Savior! Thank You for calling me, equipping me, anointing me, and choosing me for Your grand purposes. I live to make hell smaller and heaven bigger! I live to honor You with every breath, with every word, and with every minute of my life! Thank You, Father, for allowing me to teach the eternal truth that is found only in the Word of God. All the joy that I need is found in You!

> *My heart is moved with a good theme; I address my verses to the King; my tongue is the pen of a ready writer.*   —Psalm 45:1

INTRODUCTION

What an extravagant honor is yours! You have been given the unsurpassed opportunity of choosing *how* you will live the days that have been allotted to you. Although we have not been given the oversight to select the day we step from time into eternity, the power to transform *time* into a life that smacks of eternal delight has been bestowed upon us by our Creator.

You are here today, in this measured space of time, to deliver the character of God and the atmosphere of heaven into a world that seems paralyzed by pain, division, and confusion. *Today* is not a mere twenty-four-hour period; it is the ability to partner with Christ in sculpting a life of eternal significance despite the ticking of a clock, the turning of a calendar page, or the wrinkles that inevitably appear on your skin.

I can assure you that even in this space so far removed from the feast of heaven, you were created to embrace joy.

You were divinely designed to be the receptacle and the distributor of the joy of the Lord. What a glorious assignment you have been given! Each remarkable day that you live and breathe on planet Earth, you have been commissioned to demonstrate the joy of heaven's glory in the middle of Earth's pain. The astounding miracle accompanying this incredible appointment is that we, as God's children, have been allowed to carry a stunning characteristic of the Father in our human shells.

> *Splendor and majesty are before Him, strength and joy are in His place.* —1 Chronicles 16:27

COURAGEOUS RESOLVE

Often the joy of heaven is lost in the haze of earthbound living because we are jaded by disappointments, bullied by discouragement, and distracted by frustrating people. This is precisely why we need an intentional plan. A well-thought-out plan enables us to embrace the joy for which we were made. We silently but passionately hunger for a blueprint that will allow us to wring the joy out of an ordinary day. Although we don't often realize it or perhaps at times ignore it, the desperation that emotionally riles us is the deep desire to add purpose, enthusiasm, and delight to the recipe of today. Perhaps the answer lies in transforming *today* from a time period to an activity—from a noun to a verb. As you ponder this captivating possibility, maybe you would also consider making these statements of resolve:

- I will no longer tolerate today but I will participate in today.

- Today will no longer happen to me but I will happen to today.

- I refuse to merely endure today but I will enthusiastically splash today all over the gray areas of my heart.

- I will *today* joyfully and fully.

- I was made for today-ing.

We require a strategic plan that will recapture the perpetual and splendid joy for which we were divinely created. If you have been thirsty for a joy that is foreign to your personality and seems to be only a mirage in the desert of life, I hope this scintillating philosophy will stir up what has been lacking in your life. Perhaps, with me, you would be brave enough to determine to take at least one vibrant step toward the life for which you have been aching.

THE INVITATION OF PAIN

If pain has invaded your soul and trauma has deeply injured your heart, you are not excluded from this vibrant lifestyle. The decision to embrace a twenty-four-hour time period in its fullness is especially for you who have been wounded by circumstances and harassed by adversity.

I have spent many long years in the cave of depression; the anguish of personal suffering has threatened to suffocate me many times. However, I have discovered the pathway through sorrow is often made easier when I quietly but courageously *today* my way through life.

Rather than viewing pain as an obstacle to joy and therefore to abundant life, what if we viewed the unwelcome guest as an invitation to know Him more intimately? What if the troubles that formerly terrified were miraculously transformed into an avenue that led us toward Christ? I have come to believe that while joy does not deny sadness, it can often heal my heartbreak.

EACH DAY

Each chapter in this book is a reading unto itself; you can approach it as a devotional or simply as a book filled to overflowing with delight intended to revolutionize your life. At the close of each chapter are four components I hope you will linger over.

The Life Quote carries the wisdom of a man or a woman who determined to live with the fingerprint of God upon their soul. From these sage words, you might extract the strength to carry on despite what lies ahead of you, inside you, or even behind you. Perhaps you will write these words in a notebook or share them with a weary traveler in your life.

The Verse of the Day comes from the sacred pages of Scripture and is meant to confirm the lifestyle presented in the day's reading. I don't have a better idea than God, and His words are infinitely more impactful than mine! It might be a good idea to write the verse of the day in a notebook as well or even commit it to memory. If anything has the power to change your life, it is the Word of God.

The Meaningful Moment is a practical application that will help you to *today* in a purposeful manner.

The Daily Declaration are words meant to be spoken out loud at the close of each chapter. I hope you will not merely read them silently but that you will read them out loud for the host of heaven to hear.

WORTH THE INVESTMENT

As you know by now, I have this inner inkling that the word *today* should be a verb rather than a noun. As I settle upon the difference this unique belief creates in my understanding of the meaning of the word *today*, I remind myself to participate in these actions:

+ I must *today* with my whole heart.

+ I must *today* enthusiastically and enjoy the treasure that it holds.

+ I must *today* in moments of quietude rather than reflect upon the memory of yesterday.

+ I must choose to *today* even when my heart longs to sweetly rustle through the memory book of my heart.

+ I must choose to *today* when my worries about tomorrow gather in stormy clouds and obscure my view of the future.

May I just suggest that reclassification is necessary in our minds and in our hearts? Would you be willing to determine as I have that *today* is no longer a mundane noun, but a sparkling and demonstrative verb? Would you consider the option of investing yourself in making this day memorable and even celebratory? Would you roll up your sleeves and partner with God, whose very nature is joy, in establishing a life that invites others into your profound bounty of hope, generosity, and grace?

Would you respond to His delight and determine to *today* your way through life?

I can't respond for you, but I can encourage you, coach you, and even push you toward this dimension of godly living that is not for the faint of heart but for all of those who have determined their lives will smack of the atmosphere of heaven.

Behold, this is the joy of His way; and out of the dust others will spring.   —Job 8:19

The glory of God is the living man, and the life of man is
the vision of God.
—Saint Irenaeus

1

REJOICE

There is a familiar Scripture in the book of Psalms that is quoted with mundane frequency; this verse has become so commonplace we might be tempted to overlook its importance or ignore its brilliant possibilities. I have discovered in my study of Scripture over the years that often the most familiar passage holds the deepest meaning. There is a reason why recognizable verses are such a constant source of truth just as there is a reason why stability is often birthed in simplicity. Often, when our souls are aching for refreshment from the Father and for the gladness of vibrant growth, we need to reacquaint ourselves with the basics. This is one of those times.

What is the most familiar Scripture you know? Write it out here:

_____

_____

TWO SIMPLE REQUESTS

We are about to dig for sacred gold in this compact, eternal statement that comes straight from the heart of God. However, before we go on this joyful expedition, I have two simple requests for you to consider:

- Would you wipe away all preconceived ideas about these sixteen accustomed words?
- Would you determine to read this consecrated passage as if you were reading it for the very first time?

If you agree to my foundational caveats, please feel free to read on:

*This is the day the LORD has made. We will rejoice and be glad
in it.* —Psalm 118:24 NLT

What an absolute breathtaking, too-good-to-be-true wonder
is found in this verse! God has designed this distinct day especially
for you; this unique piece of time holds one primary and compelling
assignment. He has exclusively established this twenty-four-hour
period with one singular and dynamic activity outlined in His wise
mind.

In the hallways of eternity past, God incorporated a vital principle into His created blueprint labeled "Building a Life of Unmatched
Abundance." As God considered all the activities that could be
assigned to His dear children, this one is of the utmost importance.
Absolutely nothing else trumps it.

As God considered our earthly existence, He knew there would
be times when we would be desperate for the reality of delivering
heaven's glory to earth's pain. He also knew this resplendent pattern
of rejoicing daily would gird human life with an uncommon strength
and an inexpressible joy.

God, the Creator of all that is valuable and good, longs for you to
lace this day with a liberal dose of praise that deliberately rises from
the depths of your soul. He is intent on hearing your song arise from
the fierce fires in life and hearing you outsing every ferocious storm.
The Father knows what is best for you and has placed His best plans
for you on the sacred pages of Scripture. His best plan for you is to
rejoice today and every day.

WHAT IS GOD'S WILL?

Many folks wander through life wondering what God's will
might be for their incomparable yet unremarkable existence. These
searching people somehow believe God's will is a hidden mystery that
eludes a conclusive realization.

My friend, if you desire the assurance that you are participating in God's exact will for your life, it is vital to start your day with praise, then fill it to overflowing with worship and heartily end it with thanksgiving. From the first waking moment of consciousness to your last thought before sleep at night, make it a settled choice of your will to magnify the Lord. Every day that is graciously loaned to you by the Lord presents a memorable opportunity to manage your day with praise.

God's will is His specific desire for your life; God's will for the human life can also be described as the way which He deems best. You and I don't have a better idea than God does. His will is found in His Word, and we must obey His revealed will without delay.

What is your favorite worship song?

RESPONSIVE WORSHIP

As you activate your heart to experience all the glory that belongs to today, allow me to become both your cheerleader and your coach. I'd like to gently but insistently remind you that life in its exciting fullness and rich depth will never be experienced apart from responsive worship. Although the reasons why we should worship are vast and unending, perhaps these reminders will begin to stir up the song of praise only you were born to sing:

+ Worship because Jesus is Lord.

+ Worship because you have been forgiven.

+ Worship because God loves you.

+ Worship because He is worthy.

+ Worship because He hears you when you pray.

+ Worship because greater is He who is in you than he who is in the world.

The list is endless, isn't it? We could never reach the conclusion of the majestic inventory of many reasons why authentic worship should spill out of our hearts, erupt out of our mouths, and find its resting place in the throne room of God. The psalmist could not keep silent as he joyfully proclaimed all the reasons he had discovered for worshipping the Lord.

Perhaps some of these verses will instigate a grand symphony in your heart as you tether your life to the truth of God's unforgettable injunction:

I will give thanks to the LORD according to His righteousness and will sing praise to the name of the LORD Most High.
—Psalm 7:17

I will be filled with joy because of you. I will sing praises to your name, O Most High. —Psalm 9:2 NLT

And my tongue shall proclaim Your righteousness and Your praise all day long. —Psalm 35:28

My mouth is filled with Your praise and with Your glory all day long. —Psalm 71:8

List three reasons why the Lord deserves your praise every day:

1. _____

2. _____

3. _____

EVERY DAY

According to the book of Psalms, every day is a great day to break into a song of uninhibited praise. Worship holds the intrinsic power to transform a day from ordinary to meaningful and from mundane to miraculous. Will you purpose with me to awake every morning with a song brewing in your heart and then allow that bubbling melody to percolate out of your mouth?

I have unlocked immense delight while singing to the Lord in the shower even though it might sound like a raucous noise to others. While the morning is still dark and I am deciding what to clothe myself in, I whistle a holy tune. I vocalize when I wipe the kitchen counter and serenade the One who made me when I unload the dishwasher.

Worship is the metronome of life, and you must sync your heart with the One whose heart beats for you. If you ache to experience His dear presence authentically and undeniably, then you must welcome Him into your world with praise. The everydayness of life is no excuse for ignoring the invitation to worship. As you invite Him into your life with triumphant praise, He also invites you to experience His holiness and grandeur.

> But thou art holy, O thou that inhabitest the praises of Israel.
> —Psalm 22:3 WEB

When you worship the Lord, He inevitably shows up in power and in beauty. When you declare His holiness over your life, He makes Himself at home as you roll out the red carpet of praise. When you choose to rejoice in the Lord, it prepares a way for Him to rest in the splendor of your daily life. The song of your life is the welcome mat to His presence.

But the miracle isn't complete in simply knowing the Lord dwells in the song of your heart; there is another facet to sincere worship that will transform your understanding of the call to lift His name on high.

> Enter His gates with thanksgiving, and His courtyards with praise. Give thanks to Him, bless His name.   —Psalm 100:4

Do you see this? Don't miss the eternal promise that is set into motion when you belt out a tune of thanksgiving. When you choose to rejoice in the One who created you, you will receive a splendid and reciprocal invitation from the One who has listened to the love song of your heart. You, as a mortal being, are invited into the presence of a King! He instigates a royal welcome that leads into His courts as you joyfully sing your way in.

> *Enter with the password: "Thank you!" Make yourselves at home, talking praise. Thank him. Worship him.*
> —Psalm 100:4 MSG

When you build a life of heartfelt worship, He enters your life experience and sits on the throne in your heart; when you shower Him with thanksgiving, He welcomes you into His presence. What a wonderful way to spend a day—singing through every rainstorm with Him!

Can you think of a song of praise you sang as a child that still brings praise to your heart today?

LIFE QUOTE

Worship is a believer's response to God's revelation of Himself. It is expressing wonder, awe, and gratitude for the worthiness, the greatness, and the goodness of our Lord. It is the appropriate response to God's person, His provision, His power, His promises, and His plan.

—Nancy Leigh DeMoss Wolgemuth

VERSE OF THE DAY

And my tongue shall proclaim Your righteousness and Your praise all day long. —Psalm 35:28

MEANINGFUL MOMENT

Today, take the time to slow down and sing a song of praise. Sing in the shower or sing on your daily walk. Let the Lord hear your voice even though it might just sound like a joyful noise to you.

DAILY DECLARATION

"I declare that I will turn every day into a day of irrepressible rejoicing!"

2

CHOOSE

Perhaps it would be advantageous to spend just a few minutes pondering the life you hope to live. As you dream about this imagined life, intentionally remind yourself that you have been given the power of choice by your Creator. This gift of choice may just determine more aspects of your life than you care to acknowledge.

Before you question my theology or my sanity, let me share with you what I consider to be one of the most astounding and compelling verses in Scripture written, thousands of years ago:

> *My life is continually in my hand, yet I do not forget Your law.*
> —Psalm 119:109

Although the author of Psalm 119 is unnamed, most classic theologians believe that David, the giant killer who became king, wrote this Psalm. These Bible scholars also believe David likely did not write it in one sitting but over his lifetime. We cannot be certain that David wrote this glorious piece of literature but let's suppose, along with respected theological input, that David did indeed write the longest chapter in Scripture, Psalm 119.

The psalmist, who was well-acquainted with danger, enemies, and the rugged wilderness, reminds all who will listen that we choose continually what type of life we will live. This valiant man, who brought down Goliath and fought a bear with his hands, is no stranger to the complexities of life. Even though he faced a world we no longer live in today, his admonition ricochets through the hallways of time, and we must seriously consider our intentional contribution to the life we desire to live.

MY PART

As I consider other biblical heroes and heroines who faced daunting impossibilities and contended with fires, floods, and heart-break, I must remind myself that each one chose how to respond to the trauma of life.

- Noah obeyed God and built an ark during a sinful time despite ridicule.

- Esther called a fast when her entire nation was about to be slaughtered.

- Abraham took his son to the mountain and was prepared to offer him as a sacrifice.

- Daniel bowed to the Lord even though he knew the legislated consequences.

- David ran at a giant who laughed at the people of God.

- Ruth faithfully encouraged her mother-in-law and showed kindness every day after both were widowed.

How you and I respond to unthinkable situations just might determine the type of life we will live. As individuals, and as the children of God, we are often unable to control our circumstances, but we can control how we respond to those circumstances. We can respond in terror or with trust; we can react with joy or with outrage. We can choose obedience, or we can run away from the principles in Scripture. We choose.

- Like Noah, we can build a life of obedience that will protect us from the storms in life.

- Like Esther, we can choose to fast when events have escalated out of control.

- Like Abraham, we can humbly confess, "Not my will, but Your will, O Lord."

- Like Daniel, we can pray despite the disdain of the government.

- Like David, we must charge giants with an enthusiasm and boldness that comes from knowing the Father.
- And, like Ruth, we must show uncommon kindness and faithfulness even when our heart is broken.

What is the most difficult situation you have ever faced?

_____

_____

How did you respond to that situation?

_____

_____

If you had it to do over again, what would you do differently?

_____

_____

GOD'S PART

While we must choose how to respond to outrageous and unthinkable situations in life, we can also trust that our heavenly Father will never leave us or forsake us.

> *Be strong and courageous, do not be afraid or in dread of them, for the LORD your God is the One who is going with you. He will not desert you or abandon you.*   —Deuteronomy 31:6

Every reaction we choose to demonstrate must be based upon His promised presence.

- God has done His part—He has given us His promises and His presence.
- He has showered us with eternal wisdom found in Scripture.

- He has bestowed upon us the power of the Holy Spirit.
- He has forgiven our past and has offered an abundant life that none of us deserve.
- He has given us new life in Christ.
- He has loved us unconditionally and enthusiastically.

Knowing God has done His part in the outcome of your life, it will be much clearer for you to facilitate your responses to difficult days. We must make every decision based on the total assurance of God's perpetual goodness and His endless love.

What do you love most about the character of God?

How does Deuteronomy 31:6 enable you to live a life of bold conviction?

YOUR HANDS AND YOUR HEART

While the author of the amazing Psalm 119 knew that his life was in his own hands, he was also keenly aware that God's Word was in his heart and his mind. Are you also assured that the Word of God has taken its rightful place in your mind and in your heart?

We choose how we invest the hours of our days. The most important discipline you will ever embrace is to place the Word of God in your mind. You must choose to read the Word, meditate on the Word, and hide it in your heart. Nothing—absolutely nothing—will ensure that your life will be a magnificent one if you have not made room for the Bible in the priorities of life. Reading the Bible daily is not a *have to* but it is a *get to* for the man or woman who desires to live a life of untold delight and rare nobility.

You choose what will be in your heart. You choose.

Do you spend time reading your Bible every day?

———————————————————————————

———————————————————————————

How can you make room for the Word of God in your life?

———————————————————————————

———————————————————————————

LIFE QUOTE

When God comes streaming into our lives in the power of His Word, all He asks is that we be stunned and surprised, let our mouths hang open, and begin to breathe deeply.

—Brennan Manning

VERSE OF THE DAY

The Lord *is the one who is going ahead of you; He will be with you. He will not desert you or abandon you. Do not fear and do not be dismayed.* —Deuteronomy 31:8

MEANINGFUL MOMENT

Today, take the time to evaluate your life choices. Is there anything you would like to change about your life? Have you set the proper priorities in place?

DAILY DECLARATION

"I declare that I will choose God's Word and His Ways."

3

RECEIVE

Every night, when the clock strikes midnight, you are the recipient of a brand new, shining gift whose value is incalculable. Unlike the beautiful yet mistreated girl in the fairy tale, your mode of transportation will not morph into a pumpkin, nor will you be given the gift of glass slippers. However, at the stroke of this dark and inky hour, you will be given a gift so meaningful and so miraculous that even the stars twinkle in wonder. Will you receive this gift from your Creator?

YOU AND YOU ALONE

We all receive the same quantity of this prized gift regardless of weight, age, education, job description, or marital status. When each new day raises its sleepy head, you are the sole owner of 1,440 units of the most powerful commodity ever known in the history of mankind. Each day of your magnificent life, at precisely one second after midnight, heaven opens its windows and gives you 1,440 untouched and valuable minutes to spend. How you spend your minutes is entirely up to you. Perhaps you will agree that although time is free, it is also priceless.

During your 1,440, you can either gossip, or you can worship. You can choose to be filled with anger, or you can exhibit a heart overflowing with gratitude. You can jog five miles or watch television all day long. You can spend this amazing amount of time reading a book or going to the mall.

You, and you alone, determine how you will capitalize on this extravagant and priceless gift. You can choose to laugh until you cry or to cry until you ache. You might decide to whine your life away or rejoice despite your circumstances. We each determine whether our mindset and therefore our speech will be negative or positive. It is up to you to elect to be bitter or to be better.

> *Furthermore, as for every person to whom God has given riches and wealth, He has also given him the opportunity to enjoy them and to receive his reward and rejoice in his labor; this is the gift of God.*　　　　　　　　　　　　　　　—Ecclesiastes 5:19

These 1,440 precious and never to be replaced pieces of time belong to you and to no one else but you. Your spouse is not the overseer of your 1,440, your boss does not determine the value of your 1,440, and your children are not given the privilege of spending your 1,440.

What are some of the main activities that fill your 1,440?

_____

_____

Do you feel that your time is spent fulfilling the demands of others? Why or why not?

_____

_____

THE STEWARDSHIP OF OWNERSHIP

While it is true that there are demands placed upon your time, you are the one who controls *how* you accomplish those things required of you. We all deal with people who depend upon us to accomplish a long list of daily needs. However, we must respond even to demanding people with a sweet willingness to serve and a heart filled with grace.

You might maintain that the 1,440 minutes you have received are simply not enough to complete the claims that others have made on you, that even 1,880 or 2,020 would not be sufficient. However, take a deep breath and allow me to have about five of your 1,440 so I can help you shift your perspective on the gift you have been given.

As you recognize the time you have been given as a rare and meaningful gift from the Father, you must also realize that He is trusting you with the stewardship of such a gift. You must not squander nor misuse the gift of time, but you must spend every second of every day in honoring Him and encouraging others. There is simply no other or better way to live.

> I know that there is nothing better for them than to rejoice and to do good in one's lifetime; moreover, that every person who eats and drinks sees good in all his labor—this is the gift of God.
> —Ecclesiastes 3:12–13

While most of us must work, it is also true we choose *how* we will work. Will you go to the office with a chip on your shoulder and allow yourself to be filled with angst and negativity? Or will you choose to walk in with a happy heart and a solid work ethic while praying for those in your office? Certainly, you can choose to hate every minute you are at work and then waste time by participating in office gossip, playing computer games, and finally sneaking out the door five minutes early. Or you can acknowledge that God has set you in this exact environment to be a blessing to others and to bring the excellence and character of God into your workplace. You can embrace your workplace as a mission field and know that even your job is a divine appointment from the heart of the Father.

How can you turn your life into a mission field?

_____

_____

What do you believe God has placed you on earth to accomplish?

_____

_____

Will you receive His plans for your life today?

Assuredly there will be seasons in life when you must take care of aging parents, raise a brood of children, or work more hours than you desire. Nevertheless, you get to choose how to do your *have-to's*. You can march through life with heavy steps and a frustrated heart, or you can elect to perform all the necessities in life with patience, love, and joy. Even taking out the trash can become an opportunity to smile at neighbors, pull a weed or two, or whisper a prayer in the process.

THE GREATEST TRAGEDY

What is the greatest tragedy in life? Is it cancer or death? Is it bankruptcy or losing your home? I believe the greatest tragedy in life is being alive without receiving the joy of the 1,440. Certainly, the worst calamity one could ever endure may be to ignore the invitation to bask in the awareness of all that is wonderful about life.

> *God has made everything beautiful for its own time. He has planted eternity in the human heart, but even so, people cannot see the whole scope of God's work from beginning to end.*
> —Ecclesiastes 3:11 NLT

LIFE QUOTE

Serve God by doing common actions in a heavenly spirit, and then, if your daily calling only leaves you cracks and crevices of time, fill them up with holy service. —Charles Spurgeon

VERSE OF THE DAY

> *Every good thing given and every perfect gift is from above, coming down from the Father of lights, with whom there is no variation or shifting shadow.*   —James 1:17

MEANINGFUL MOMENT

Make a list of how you are spending your 1,440. Do this over the course of a week and then evaluate your time commitments.

DAILY DECLARATION

"I declare today that I will not waste my 1,440 but I will use my minutes to honor the Lord and to encourage others."

4

CELEBRATE!

We serve a heavenly Father who is an extravagant and intentional gift-giver. He gives gifts on purpose and has not ignored one of us when it comes to the giving of extraordinary gifts.

There are many gifts listed in Scripture; each of these biblical gifts was given to ensure that the children of God would live an abundant life. Perhaps, as you read the passage below, you will recognize a gift the Lord has given specifically to you:

> *Since we have gifts that differ according to the grace given to us, each of us is to use them properly: if prophecy, in proportion to one's faith; if service, in the act of serving; or the one who teaches, in the act of teaching; or the one who exhorts, in the work of exhortation; the one who gives, with generosity; the one who is in leadership, with diligence; the one who shows mercy, with cheerfulness.* —Romans 12:6–8

There are other places in Scripture that require us to consider the gifts given by the Holy Spirit:

> *Now there are varieties of gifts, but the same Spirit. And there are varieties of ministries, and the same Lord. There are varieties of effects, but the same God who works all things in all persons. But to each one is given the manifestation of the Spirit for the common good. For to one is given the word of wisdom through the Spirit, and to another the word of knowledge according to the same Spirit; to another faith by the same Spirit, and to another gifts of healing by the one Spirit, and to another the effecting of miracles, and to another prophecy, and to another the distinguishing of spirits, to another various kinds of tongues, and to another the interpretation of tongues. But one and the same*

Spirit works all these things, distributing to each one individually just as He wills. —1 Corinthians 12:4–11

As you read these Scriptures, can you identify a gift the Lord has given to you?

_____

_____

How do these gifts guarantee abundant life?

_____

_____

IT'S A GIFT!

Everyone will share the story of your wonderful goodness; they will sing with joy about your righteousness.

—Psalm 145:7 NLT

I have always wondered if the generous and infinite heavenly Father had more gifts to give than just those listed in the Bible. Certainly, the ones referenced in Scripture are the most vital and prioritized gifts, but as I ponder the broad character of God, I wonder if He has other gifts up His heavenly sleeve. Perhaps these other gifts could be listed under the categories of *talents* or even *personality preferences*, but they are gifts nonetheless.

I have quietly yet perpetually contemplated if *celebration* was one of my assigned gifts. Although everyone who knows me would never ascribe the phrase *party girl* to my persona, I do have a knack for celebrating ordinary days in rare and memorable style. I have found that this penchant for celebration has become a habitual lifestyle and is a captivating aspect of who I am to my core.

+ On March 17, I serve green mashed potatoes to my family.

- On April Fool's Day, we have spaghetti for breakfast and pancakes for dinner.

- March Madness is a holiday complete with trophies, T-shirts, and the giving of gifts.

- October 1 is the first official day of Christmas music season.

- My Thanksgiving celebration is not just a day, but it is a way of life.

- I consider it to be a good day if I have laughed, forgiven, and smiled.

When I was a young bride, I spent time with an older woman who seemed to have this same propensity for celebrating the life she had been given. One day as we were sitting together, enjoying a cup of English tea, I wondered out loud if I would ever actually use the fine china that had been given to me as wedding gifts. Her immediate reply, with a sparkle in her Dutch blue eyes was this, "Carol, don't ever save anything for a special occasion. Being alive *is* the special occasion."

I have tried to follow this wise advice every day of my life.

What are some of the ways in which you celebrate an ordinary day?

_____

_____

What is your favorite holiday?

_____

_____

EVERYTHING I KNOW

My mother is quite the woman and has certainly learned the fine art of how to make a grand entrance. Several years ago, the entrance she made one Easter weekend was one of the grandest of all.

Mom arrived at my home on Good Friday afternoon with bags overflowing with goodies from the Amish bakery. I am not exaggerating. There were eight boxes filled with scrumptious blueberry pie, pumpkin bread, peanut butter cookies, coconut cake, pecan rolls—an Easter parade of various and colorful desserts. I could nearly feel the pounds packing on my middle-aged body as I merely sniffed the delicious mounds of sugared confections placed on my kitchen counter.

She also ushered in two shopping bags filled with her used, designer purses and wondered if either I or my daughters would enjoy them. Enjoy them? Designer purses that had only been used once or twice?! Let us at them!

She also brought three shopping bags packed to the rim with shoes, still in their boxes and never worn. My mom has a delightful habit of buying shoes a half size too small for her feet, but they just happen to miraculously fit mine! Her excessive shopping habits have blessed my closet for decades.

She handed each of the boys a $20 bill and gave each girl a piece of heirloom jewelry. As I said, my mom knows how to make quite an unforgettable entrance.

After we each devoured a peanut butter cookie straight from the heart of Amish country, the matriarch of our family gathered everyone around the island in my kitchen. She wanted to read something she had written that day while on the five-hour car trip from her home to ours. Of course, we all obediently gathered, and the family grew quiet. We have learned over the years that when Mimi speaks, what comes out of her mouth is pure treasure.

She drew a piece of paper from her designer purse and first read us the title she had given to this masterpiece, "Things I Love." She then cleared her throat, with her eyes sparkling, and read with great enthusiasm the list of all the things in life that she loves.

THINGS I LOVE

Hot baths

Two-year-olds

Houses on hills

Pretty hairdos

Laughter

Chocolate

Children who rave about their parents

Yellow daffodils

Hometowns

Lattes

Pumpkin pie

Lines in the carpet

Luxurious vacations

Happy husbands

Sparkling windows

Rides in the country

Sunday afternoons

Positive people

Love stories

Diamonds

Blue skies

Old ladies *(of which she is most certainly not one!)*

Picturesque churches

Immaculate houses

Purses *(who could have guessed?!)*

Loyal friends

My mom has learned the eternal secret of gratitude and celebration. She is a licensed expert on how to celebrate an ordinary day. My mom's life has been far from perfect and yet she maintains an enthusiasm for life that is hers and hers alone. My mom pirouettes through all the minutes of her life while singing at the top of her vibrant lungs. I want to be just like my mom.

What are some of the memories you hold of your mother?

If your childhood was unhappy, what have you done to create a better life for those you love?

LIFE QUOTE

Tell me, what is it you plan to do with your one wild and precious life?   —Mary Oliver

VERSE OF THE DAY

*Now this day shall be a memorial to you, and you shall **celebrate** it as a feast to the LORD; throughout your generations you are to **celebrate** it as a permanent ordinance.*   —Exodus 12:14

MEANINGFUL MOMENT

Make a list of the things you love like my mother did. Share it with someone today.

DAILY DECLARATION

"I declare that from this day forward, I will wring the joy out of an ordinary day."

5

ENCOURAGE

Do you remember the last time someone criticized you? Do you recall the instant pain—even the recoiling from wanting to continue a relationship with this person? This conversation may have taken place years ago and yet still you remember the feeling and the words as if it happened yesterday.

Conversely, do you remember a time during your childhood when a teacher, a parent, or a friend encouraged you? I still remember the exact words today—nearly six decades later—that my kindergarten teacher spoke to me as an impressionable five-year-old. Her words have lived on and on in my heart.

I attended a one-room schoolhouse and my beloved first teacher was Mrs. Dombrowski, an Australian war bride. Although she was childless, she loved each one of us as if we were her very own. I was eavesdropping on the spelling lesson she had been teaching to the third graders because I had quickly finished my seat work. Mrs. Dombrowski knew I had been listening and quietly called me to her desk. She then asked me to spell the words *elephant* and *hippopotamus*. I was able to do so because I had absorbed the entire lesson just given to the group of children who were three years older than me. Mrs. Dombrowski looked me straight into my eyes and said, "Carol, I expect great things from you. Don't waste what God has given to you."

The reality is that our words can change someone's life. Our words travel through time and hit the target of a person's heart again and again and again.

Who has been a source of encouragement in your life?

_____

_____

How have discouraging words impacted your life?

_____

_____

IF IT'S TODAY

We have been strategically fashioned by our Creator to need the encouragement that comes from others. It is not enough to encourage your spouse, a friend, a parent, or a child once a week; the Bible is clear that encouragement is meant to be a continual action.

> But **encourage** one another every day, as long as it is still called "today," so that none of you will be hardened by the deceitfulness of sin. —Hebrews 3:13

If you can look at your calendar and discern it is *today*, then you are invited by the holy Scriptures to use your tongue as a tool of warm and sincere encouragement. Is it today? Then your assignment is easy and obvious: you get to be an encourager!

The word for "encourage" used in this unforgettable verse is a compound of the Greek words *para* and *kaleo*. The word *para* means "alongside" and *kaleo* means "to call, to speak, or to beckon." Therefore, the Greek word *parakaleo* "gives the picture of someone who has come closely alongside of another person for the sake of speaking to him, consoling him, comforting him, or assisting him."[1]

+ When in doubt, encourage someone.

+ When a relationship is unraveling, encourage this person.

---

1. Rick Renner, *Sparkling Gems from the Greek, Volume I* (Broken Arrow, OK: Teach All Nations, 2003), 464.

- If someone has offended you, encourage this person anyway.

- If someone is discouraged, choose to be an encourager.

- Encourage those who are older than you are.

- Encourage someone who is younger than you are.

- Look into a child's face and tell this little one how simply amazing he or she is.

The verb tense utilized in this particular verse calls for a continual action. Therefore, we, as the body of Christ, are called to a lifestyle of encouragement. Encouragement is not just something you do but it is who you are to your very core.

What are three adjectives that describe your character?

_____

_____

Do you have a difficult person in your life? How can you encourage this person?

_____

_____

YOUR TONGUE AND YOUR HEART

It is of utmost importance to understand why the Lord equipped you with a tongue in your human body. You were not given a tongue to spew forth negativity, to criticize others made in the image of God, or to gossip. I believe our tongues were created for three God-given purposes:

- We were given a tongue to praise the Lord every minute of every day.

- We were given a tongue to declare the Word and will of God over our lives.

• We were given a tongue to encourage others.

It is absurd to think we might use a wrench to sign our names, utilize a pair of scissors to open a can of vegetables, or rev up the lawn mower when it is time to vacuum our carpets. Perhaps it's just as preposterous when we use our tongues to spread a rumor, as a weapon of intimidation, or to flagrantly make fun of someone.

When our tongues are solely used for their God-given purpose, they become a powerful pen writing a beautiful story, a valuable paintbrush creating a masterpiece, and a melodic score of rare and lush music.

It's not only your tongue that you must use as an agent of encouragement, but your heart must also be a deep well from which you draw pure thoughts and loving words. When you feel judgment stirring the waters of your heart, make a quick decision to bless that person instead. When the murky mud of criticism endeavors to live in the cistern of your soul, clear it away with the purity of Scripture.

You were given a tongue to encourage others and a heart with which to love others. My friend, please don't use these two crucial components of your humanity for any other purpose at all.

THINK ABOUT IT

Perhaps it would be a productive exercise to think about the time when someone offered to pay for your lunch, brought you a meal, or spoke of you to others in a kind manner. What a gift it is when someone generously offers the gift of encouragement, whether by words or by acts of service!

If you are feeling as if you are the one who needs to be encouraged, let me challenge you to be the encourager instead. When you encourage someone verbally, financially, or through service, your endorphin levels will rise. Endorphins are the hormones that help you battle depression, discouragement, and emotional malaise. As you choose to encourage someone, the blessing will come back to you in generous amounts.

When your lifestyle of encouragement collides with someone who is lonely or disheartened, you will change their life. You will usher health and healing into the atmosphere that surrounds them. You will be giving them the oxygen of hope and restored joy.

My friend, when you are an encourager, you become the most powerful version of yourself possible.

LIFE QUOTE

If I can put one touch of a rosy sunset into the life of any man or woman ... I shall feel that I have worked with God.

—George MacDonald

VERSE OF THE DAY

Therefore, **encourage** *one another and build one another up, just as you also are doing.*   —1 Thessalonians 5:11

MEANINGFUL MOMENT

Pause and pray for just a moment. Ask the Lord to show you who needs your encouragement today, this week, and this month. Write down their names and then intentionally look for opportunities to share a word of encouragement with each one of them.

DAILY DECLARATION

"I declare that I was given a tongue by my Creator to encourage everyone in my life."

6

FORGIVE

I have long believed the word *forgiveness* is the most endearing yet dynamic word in the entire English language. *Forgiveness* is not for the small of mind nor for the selfish in heart, but it is a word that invites us to become like Christ.

In this journey of life on earth, you will encounter many people who will wound you, betray you, condemn you, judge you, and hurt you. As one who has experienced the freedom of forgiveness, our instant response to these burdensome people should be immediate and thorough forgiveness.

We rub shoulders daily with prickly folks who are oblivious to our feelings, destroy our self-esteem, and seem intent on policing our every move. Our instinctive reaction to these unaware and fractious humans should be generous and gracious forgiveness.

Who has hurt you the most deeply in life? Have you forgiven this person?

_____

_____

Before you read any further, write your own definition of the word "forgiveness."

_____

_____

UNDESERVING

I don't know what pain you carry in your heart due to mistreatment from others, but I am aware that most of us plod through life never truly processing the pain of emotional injury in a godly, healthy manner. We have mistakenly believed that giving the silent treatment, allowing anger to simmer for years, or ignoring the wound is the correct response. We have thought that lashing out, yelling, or slamming doors would somehow make us feel better.

> *So, as those who have been chosen of God, holy and beloved, put on a heart of compassion, kindness, humility, gentleness, and patience; bearing with one another, and forgiving each other, whoever has a complaint against anyone; just as the Lord forgave you, so must you do also.* —Colossians 3:12–13

As I study Scripture, I have come to the realization that the Lord has only one answer for the persecution we have endured at the hands of others. His answer is forgiveness—complete and total forgiveness.

I have wrestled with the incongruity of this difficult yet godly response nearly my entire life. Have you? I have often believed that those who have abused or bullied me didn't *deserve* my forgiveness. The Holy Spirit has been gentle with me over this delicate issue as I am sure He will be with you. The Holy Spirit, also known in Scripture as "the Comforter," has assured me that at the very heart of forgiveness is the complexity that it is undeserved. If someone *deserved* your forgiveness, they wouldn't need to be forgiven, would they?

+ Forgiveness is when the innocent one lets the guilty one go free.

+ The whole point of forgiveness is that it is undeserved.

+ Forgiveness is not casual but intentional.

+ Forgiveness invites us to enter the wonderful arena of new beginnings.

+ Forgiveness does not change your past, but it does change your future.

WHAT WOULD JESUS DO?

Our one assignment during our tenure on earth is to become like Jesus. If we truly took that assignment seriously, it would impact every area of life. We would worship God in spirit and in truth, we would hear the voice of the Father, we would show unconditional love, we would pray for the sick and honor the Scriptures. Perhaps there is no other area of paramount importance in our journey to become like Jesus than that of forgiveness.

> *For if you forgive other people for their offenses, your heavenly Father will also forgive you. But if you do not forgive other people, then your Father will not forgive your offenses.*
> —Matthew 6:14–15

Jesus came to earth to forgive our sins and to reveal the heart of the Father to us. As our lives become hidden with God in Jesus Christ, we must willfully choose to forgive the difficult people in our lives. Forgiveness is part of the family business, and we must represent our Father joyfully and willingly.

When it seems achingly difficult to forgive someone who has hurt you or who has betrayed someone you love, ask the Father to give you the desire and the strength to become like Jesus. This is an area in life where we must lay down our will for the greater will of the Father. We must say a resounding *yes* to God and a humble *no* to our flesh. Although I might not *want* to forgive a person, I do want to become like Jesus. I want to be like Jesus more than I want to be like me, get my own way or fight my own battles.

I remind myself daily that I don't have a better idea than God. God has the best ideas in all of eternity past and in all of eternity yet to come. Forgiveness has always been—and will always be—one of God's very best ideas.

Is it more difficult to forgive yourself or someone who has wronged you? Why?

_____

_____

Is it more difficult to forgive someone who has wronged you or someone who has hurt someone you love? Why?

_____

_____

A GIFT

Forgiveness is a rare and valuable gift given to those whose lives have cruelly collided with your unprotected heart. Forgiveness often must begin with a declaration that is largely unfelt emotionally. However, as you and I make the determination to act like Christ regardless of the personal cost, the stubbornness that keeps us from desiring to forgive the aggressor will soon begin to melt away. We will quickly realize the gift of forgiveness is also a gift of glorious freedom.

Humbly, we will ascertain that not only were we the giver of the gift but the recipient as well. This is what I call a *glorious conundrum*. We give and yet we receive; we die and yet we live. We forgive, and we are set free. As you forgive someone who doesn't deserve it, you will suddenly realize that it is the best gift you have ever given to yourself.

LIFE QUOTE

To be a Christian means to forgive the inexcusable, because God has forgiven the inexcusable in you.   —C. S. Lewis

VERSE OF THE DAY

Be kind to one another, compassionate, forgiving each other, just as God in Christ also has forgiven you.   —Ephesians 4:32

MEANINGFUL MOMENT

Pause to pray for a minute. Ask the Lord if you have allowed unforgiveness against a person to build in your heart. Give yourself the gift of choosing to forgive this person completely. Today.

DAILY DECLARATION

"I declare that I will forgive lavishly, generously, and completely because Christ has forgiven me."

7

PRAY

How wonderful to know we have been warmly invited into the throne room of God almighty to speak with Him on a minute-by-minute basis! How wonderful to know that He hears us when we pray. And how wonderful to comprehend we usher the fullness of heaven to earth when we simply lift our hearts and our voices in prayer. How wonderful!

> *You have been cordially invited*
> *by the King of all kings,*
> *the Creator of heaven and earth,*
> *to spend time in His holy and joyful presence.*

WHY PRAY?

Prayer was always meant to be the outflow of relationship with the Father; prayer is time set aside to focus on who He is and on the glory that belongs to His name.

The most well-known Scripture concerning prayer is from a conversation Jesus had with His disciples one day. These young men, called personally by Jesus to follow Him, observed how He prayed and could not help but ask Him to teach them to pray. I've always thought it interesting that the disciples didn't ask Jesus to teach them to preach, or how to fast effectively, or even how to heal someone, but they asked Him how to pray. Perhaps this would be a good question for us to ask Jesus as well. The Lord's Prayer is the prototype prayer for Christians from all millennia and from around the globe:

> *After this manner therefore pray ye: Our Father who art in*
> *heaven, hallowed be thy name. Thy kingdom come. Thy will be*

*done on earth as [it is] in heaven. Give us this day our daily
bread. And forgive us our debts, as we forgive our debtors. And
lead us not into temptation, but deliver us from evil. For thine is
the kingdom, and the power, and the glory, for ever. Amen.*
—Matthew 6:9–13 WEB

Knowing that prayer is one of the most powerful and dynamic
choices one can make daily, why do we not pray?

+ Why do we watch TV rather than pray?

+ Why do we scroll social media rather than pray?

+ Why do we engage in meaningless activities rather than pray?

+ Why do we allow our minds to wander far away from the
  throne room of God?

+ Why do we refuse to position our hearts in an attitude of prayer?

+ Why?

Paul, in his letter to the Philippians, invites Christians to pray
about everything and let every request be made known to God. (See
Philippians 4:6.) We must develop a mentality in which we are turning everything in our lives over to God in prayer.

Any area of your life of your life that you choose not to pray
about is an area in which you are saying, "God, I don't need You. I can
handle this on my own."

*Who has prayed for you in your life's journey? Stop and pray for this
person today.*

_____

_____

*Make a list of at least three people whom you have been assigned to
pray for.*

_____

_____

HELP!

He who did not spare His own Son, but delivered Him over for us all, how will He not also with Him freely give us all things?
—Romans 8:32

One of the primary purposes of prayer is to ask God for help. We are human, and He is divine—where else would we go for help? Jesus wants to be engaged in our lives; we can ask Him and He will step in and move if we only just cry out for help.

God loves you enough that He wants to help you with your *big* stuff and your *small* stuff. The truth is, nothing is *big* from God's point of view. Nothing is too big for God to handle, and nothing is too small for Him to care about. He can handle every cry for help you will ever whisper, shout, or cry. So, pray on. God cares about the details of your ordinary life. If it matters to you, it matters to God.

You do not have because you do not ask.   —James 4:2

God wants to lighten your load, but you must invite His strength into your weakness. He longs to hear your voice and for you just to ask Him for His magnificent help. God requires you to ask Him for what only He is able to do.

The Lord requires our own acknowledgment of our personal needs. Praying and asking is not a demand of a selfish child but it opens the windows of heaven for God's grace to flood into our pain and helplessness. When a child of God is on his or her knees in desperation for the intervention of God, this posture of humility and helplessness communicates dependence upon our Father and trust that He will do what is right.

What is the greatest answer to prayer you have ever experienced?

_____

_____

What are some of your distractions when it comes to being committed to prayer?

_____

_____

EVEN JESUS

Praying is a kingdom act of obedience; even Jesus was required to pray to His Father. If Jesus, the Son of God, was compelled to pray, how much more vital it is for you and me to lift up our voices to God, our good, good Father.

Jesus prayed often throughout His earthly life. He had to ask of the Lord to receive what He needed as a man. Jesus prayed on the mountain, and He prayed in the boat; Jesus prayed in the garden, and He prayed in the wilderness. Jesus prayed with others, and He prayed alone. If you want to be just like Jesus, you will bend your knee, humble your heart, and pray.

Praying is relational; God the Father longs to have a relationship with you. One of the ways relationship is accomplished is through the sweet connection that only happens in prayer. God is not a Santa Claus in the sky who magically throws down blessings independent of a heart-to-heart connection with Him. He wants us to bring our needs to Him because He loves us.

Pray on, my beloved sister and my courageous brother. Confess your dependence on the Father and cry out to Him in heartfelt supplication. If your soul is in need, you have come to the right place. Seeking God's help for every circumstance in life will sustain you, strengthen you, and give you the wisdom only He can provide. When you acknowledge reliance in prayer upon all that He is, He will answer with His power and His grace. God only comes where He is welcome, and He waits to answer until He is called.

The most powerful choice you will ever make on any day of your life is to pray. As you pray, you will deliver His unshakable kingdom to your moment in history. When you pray, you become a co-laborer with God to impact human history.

If you could ask the Lord one question, what would it be?

_____

_____

LIFE QUOTE

Prayer changes hearts but it never changes God. God is the same today and forever, full of love, full of entreaty, full of helpfulness.   —Smith Wigglesworth

VERSE OF THE DAY

Let my prayer come before You; incline Your ear to my cry!
                                        —Psalm 88:2

MEANINGFUL MOMENT

Do you have a prayer journal? Today might be a good day to begin the practice of writing down your prayer requests and then also make a notation when each request is answered.

DAILY DECLARATION

"I declare that I will begin every day with prayer and end every day with prayer, knowing He is only a whisper away."

8

PERSEVERE

Life can be unbearably hard; there are seasons in life when disappointment bullies us and discouragement robs our strength. For each one of us, there comes a moment of decision in the midst of a ferocious trial. A trial forces us to determine if we will give up, give in, or give all.

Perseverance is the ability to press on with resolution despite the opposition standing in the way. Perseverance is a little bit grit, a good measure of determination, and a mountain of faith. One's journey in life might not always be easy or predictable, but perseverance is the only virtue that will enable you to carry on with joy.

What is the most difficult situation you have ever gone through in life?

_____

_____

If you had it to do over again, what would you do differently?

_____

_____

PERSEVERING IN FAITH

The Lord never promised an easy road this side of heaven. However, He did promise He would willingly and generously give us the strength to go through every difficulty in life.

I can do all things through Him who strengthens me.
—Philippians 4:13

While it is true that we might face persecution, rejection, failure, loneliness, health issues, and a host of other battles, we must use these challenges as a springboard for courage. When we are filled with the bravery that only comes from the Lord, we are able to develop an attitude of perseverance.

When trials relentlessly pursue us, there are times we might be tempted to question God's goodness, His love, His promises, His faithfulness, or His authority. In those moments, we must fix our eyes on Jesus rather than on the storm that is swirling around us.

> *Therefore, since we also have such a great cloud of witnesses surrounding us, let's rid ourselves of every obstacle and the sin which so easily entangles us, and let's run with endurance the race that is set before us, looking only at Jesus, the originator and perfecter of the faith, who for the joy set before Him endured the cross, despising the shame, and has sat down at the right hand of the throne of God.* —Hebrews 12:1–2

We will never have the stamina to persevere in our own strength; we are in desperate need of a power greater than our own. This power is delivered into our very lives as we keep our eyes on Jesus, as we stand in strong faith, and as we refuse to grow weary in well-doing.

> *Let us not be weary in well-doing: for in due season we shall reap, if we faint not.* —Galatians 6:9 WEB

What does it mean to you to "not be weary in well-doing"?

_____

_____

What are some of the challenges that cause you to grow weary?

_____

_____

GOD CALLS

God calls His beloved children, at every moment in history, to be men and women of great resolve. He calls us to be men and women who will face the future and our destiny with a determination that causes hell to shake and heaven to rise to its feet with a rousing cheer. Our call is that nothing—absolutely nothing—will take us from our course in life. We must make the unalterable determination that not one thing will distract, detour, or disrupt us from our course in Christ Jesus.

What has God called you to do? Have you heard His voice calling you to do something you know is impossible to accomplish on your own? What will you do with that human impossibility?

- Has God called you to raise children for His glory?
- Has He called you to support missions or to go on short-term missions' trips?
- Has He asked you to build a business known for its integrity?
- Has He tapped you to run for public office? To write a book?
- Has He put the dream in your heart to lead thousands in worship?
- Has He appointed you to be a light in the marketplace?

There is a call on each one of our lives, requiring relentless perseverance and resolute determination. Your call is likely the last thought you ponder before you drift off to sleep at night and your very first thought in the early morning hours. When you discover your purpose, be unstoppable in the pursuit! Refuse to back off, grow weary, or give in. Do not allow the devil or the world to inform you what you can or cannot do. We get our marching orders from the Word of God and from the throne room of heaven; nothing will cause us to stop or pause in the march.

If you could do anything for the kingdom of God, what would it be?

What will it take to accomplish this call? List some practical steps.

1. _____

2. _____

3. _____

4. _____

5. _____

A RELENTLESS MAN

Paul was a man who was determined to be relentless in his pursuit of Christ and in his call to make a resounding difference at his given moment in God's history book. The Holy Spirit had called Paul to go to Jerusalem and warned him that trials would await him there. These are the words of a persistent man of God written nearly two thousand years ago:

> And now behold, I go bound in the spirit to Jerusalem, not knowing the things that shall befall me there: save that the Holy Spirit testifieth in every city, saying, that bonds and afflictions abide me. **But none of these things move me,** neither count I my life dear to myself, so that I may finish my course with joy, and the ministry which I have received from the Lord Jesus, to testify the gospel of the grace of God.   —Acts 20:22–24 WEB

Paul declared with sober enthusiasm that nothing moved him from the course God had laid out for him. Paul understood what it would take to follow the leading of the Lord wholeheartedly and with every breath he took.

It is inevitable that many distractions will try to move us from the course of our God-given destiny. For some, it is financial challenges; for others, it is difficult people. Infertility can be devastating, and living the life of a single man or woman may be filled with loneliness.

The Holy Spirit is looking for men and women in every generation who refuse to be moved from what the Father has called them to.

What are the distractions that have endeavored to move you from the course of your God-given destiny?

_____

_____

_____

_____

What can you do in a practical sense to ignore the distractions and fulfill your calling in Christ?

_____

_____

One of the most amazing statements Paul makes is that he is steadfast in his decision to finish his race with joy.

+ Paul knew that he would be persecuted ... but he would hold on to his joy.

+ Paul knew that religious leaders would mock him ... but he would hold on to his joy.

+ Paul knew he might be thrown into prison ... but he would hold on to his joy.

What does it mean to you to "hold on to your joy"?

_____

_____

Paul was a man of unique and admirable perseverance. His single-minded, sold-out desire was to finish his race well and with joy. I have declared for years that I will cross my finish line sweaty rather than rusty. I may be out of breath and have no human strength remaining as I cross from time into eternity, but I will stubbornly and passionately persevere and cross my finish line with joy.

What is your one desire?

_____

_____

LIFE QUOTE

Endurance is the ability to weather a trial without resorting to sinful means of deliverance.   —Lou Priolo

VERSE OF THE DAY

Be on the alert, stand firm in the faith, act like men, be strong.
                              —1 Corinthians 16:13

MEANINGFUL MOMENT

Make a list of three to five things you are determined to accomplish before you move to heaven. Pray over this list daily and do whatever it takes to accomplish these goals.

DAILY DECLARATION

"I declare that I will cross my finish line sweaty not rusty!"

9

SMILE

How I loved my Aunt Marianne, affectionately known as *Auntie* to a host of children who lived in our small town in mid-century America. Auntie was a beloved elementary school teacher who was admired and respected by adults, teens, and children alike. She and her dear husband, my wonderful Uncle Doug, were unable to have biological children, so they adopted my three adored cousins, Joy, Paul, and Anne.

Auntie read *Pippi Longstocking* and *Caddie Woodlawn* to me on long summer afternoons while we sat in her hammock underneath the shade of the elm tree in her backyard. She was my first piano teacher, my first church choir director, and one of my Latin teachers. Auntie taught me to love the written word, choral music, and molasses cookies. In the second grade, when my teacher was concerned about my penmanship, my mother sent me to Auntie's house every Saturday morning to learn how to form my letters correctly and beautifully. It's a gift I don't take for granted even today.

As the years passed by, and Auntie entered her last decade of life this side of eternity, she began to lose her effervescent memory. She talked about children's books to people in the grocery store, was no longer able to find her way home from her teaching assignments, and voraciously gathered up the condiments in restaurants, hiding them in her oversized purse. Although Auntie could no longer hold meaningful conversations and had forgotten most of what she had learned, she knew how to smile. She would repeat to everyone she encountered, "If someone has lost a smile, give him one of yours."

What teacher or family member from your childhood impacted you greatly?

_____

_____

What did you love or appreciate the most about this person?

_____

_____

IT'S FREE!

I don't have a lot to offer the people in my life in terms of money, material wealth, or generous donations. However, I can give everyone I meet a smile, an encouraging word, and a positive heart attitude. When I give a genuine and sincere smile to someone, it doesn't cost me anything, but it gives something rare and priceless.

+ A smile can turn a bad day into a good day.

+ A smile can fight off depression and weariness of the soul.

+ A smile is another way of saying, "I see you. You are important."

+ A smile is a gift to the one who sees it, and it makes the giver even more attractive.

+ When you smile at the world, it smiles back at you in return.

+ If you want to change the world, just smile at a stranger.

+ A smile has unseen power to cure the afflictions of almost any soul.

One of the most wonderful byproducts of smiling at a stranger, a friend, or even an acquaintance is that it grows and even explodes. When you smile at someone, they are likely to smile back and then smile at someone else. The best smiles turn into greetings and warm conversations. A smile is able to diffuse a whimper and bolster frayed nerves. A smile is one of the loveliest of gifts to offer, a gift that will sustain your own heart through loneliness and insecurity.

Who is the happiest, most cheerful person you know?

_____

_____

What makes this person cheerful?

_____

_____

Has this person lived a trouble-free life?

_____

_____

A COMPLETE MAKE-OVER

When I was a teenager and the grumpiness of adolescence was pasted on my countenance, my mother would quietly whisper in my ear, "Fix your face." She wasn't instructing me to wipe a piece of neglected food from my chin, nor was she reminding me to powder my nose, but she was gently yet firmly reminding me to smile. My mom knew the intrinsic and natural beauty that was given with just a simple smile. She also wanted me to realize that my smile could change someone else's day—and so can yours.

A smile will do for you what make-up is unable to do; a smile adds genuine and natural beauty that nothing else has the power to enhance.

Do you believe that simply smiling at someone could change their life? Why or why not?

_____

_____

What other simple acts can we give to others that just might change their life?

_____

_____

A smile is, quite simply, nothing less than a bona fide miracle in the making. You see, if you don't *feel* like smiling, but decide to smile anyway, your heart begins to lift. A smile is able to make weariness flee and insecurities vanish. As you continue to smile as an act of generosity and selflessness, you will change in the process. Your heart not only lifts in response to the smile, but it begins to join in the facial celebration. Your heart now becomes the instigator of the smiling process; inwardly, you become renewed and refreshed.

I have long known that a smile not only encourages the person who receives it, but it also changes the one who gives it. Isn't it interesting that a smile is not only shaped like a boomerang, but it often acts like one too? Just as a boomerang returns to the sender, so does a smile.

THE FUTURE AND YOU

There are many things that deny us of the simple delight of smiling, but among the most adversarial are the worries and cares of tomorrow. When we have our heart in tomorrow and our feet in today, there are no smiles to be conjured up, to be fabricated, or to be revealed. Worry and anxiety cause us to wear an ugly mask of our own choosing; fret becomes a frown and dread is dastardly.

The devil is intent on convincing you not to enjoy today and one of the ways he does this is by persuading you that you will not be able to handle the uncertainty of tomorrow. The devil does not want to see you smile because he knows the inherent power a smile holds for you and for others. If you can keep your heart focused on the rare enchantment that belongs only to today and trust God with all your tomorrows, the enemy will no longer own your face or your heart.

Whenever I read the description of the incomparable woman of God in Proverbs 31, I always feel as if I will never meet her high standard. She is Miss America, Mother Teresa, and Joanna Gaines all wrapped up into one exceptional package. However, when my eyes light upon this verse, I know that I am in good company with this heroine from the Bible:

She smiles at the future.   —Proverbs 31:25

Smiling might be the only thing I have in common with her, but I am determined to out-smile this dignified woman of old.

+ I might never make a million dollars ... but I can smile.
+ I might never be president ... but I can smile.
+ I might never win an Olympic medal ... but I can smile.
+ I might never preach to millions ... but I can smile.

LIFE QUOTE

God loves you and He has not forgotten you. You have a reason to smile.   —Eric Nyamekye

VERSE OF THE DAY

Servants, respectfully obey your earthly masters but always with an eye to obeying the real master, Christ. Don't just do what you have to do to get by, but work heartily, as Christ's servants doing what God wants you to do. And work with a smile on your face, always keeping in mind that no matter who happens to be giving the orders, you're really serving God. Good work will get you good pay from the Master, regardless of whether you are slave or free.   —Ephesians 6:5–8 MSG

MEANINGFUL MOMENT

You must make smiling part of your daily routine—you simply must! Resolve to smile at strangers, at people you meet daily, and at your dearest of friends.

DAILY DECLARATION

"I declare that I will smile at strangers and at children; I will smile outside and inside. I will smile in public and in private. I will *fix my face* and in doing so, I just might change the world!"

10

FORGET

Several years ago, as I was reading the Bible, I realized there are times in Scripture when we, as God's children, are instructed to *forget*. However, a riddle was born in that moment because I know there are other places in the Word of God that tell us to *remember*. Was I supposed to forget? Or was I supposed to remember? I was in a conundrum of the most challenging kind—an enigma instigated by Scripture!

I decided to spend the next few months doing a word study on these two contradictory words, *forget* and *remember*. After hours of study and prayer, I understood that solving this sacred stumper was much simpler than I had first supposed. The obvious and evident truth I have found in Scripture is this: I am supposed to forget *my* stuff and remember God's stuff.

I must not forget to *remember* Him and all that He has done. I must also remember to *forget* all that is unnecessary to my walk in Christ.

What has been the most difficult event for you to forget in life?

_____

_____

If you could do one thing over again, what would it be?

_____

_____

IT SHOULD NOT BE SO

It is extremely challenging to forget all my failures, my past pain, and my difficult memories. It is even more difficult to lay these putrid parts of yesterday at the foot of the cross of Christ and leave them there. Unfortunately, I must admit there are times when I long to desperately hold on to those things that tie me to the inequity of life on the *time side* of eternity. I am not proud to admit that I often enjoy a good roll in the sludge of awful memories, unrighteous behavior, and the rejection of others. Why do I want to do that to myself? The answer is obvious—it is because I am human.

It is a part of our humanity that choosing to remember the unpleasant happenings of yesterday somehow justifies our weaknesses and failures. There is a certain thrill that jolts us into a twisted energy when we talk about how we were mistreated, how sick we were, or how difficult life used to be. But it should not be so, my brothers and my sisters. It should not be so.

When Joseph, one of the heroes of the Old Testament, had a son after years spent in captivity and in prison, he named him *Manasseh*, which means "to forget," because *"God has made me forget all my trouble and all my father's household"* (Genesis 41:51). Joseph refused to allow his past pain to torment him in his new life. Often, we do just that, don't we? We bring the troubles of yesterday into today and thereby keep them alive long after their expiration date. A stronger, even healthier choice is to keep the past in the past and remember it no longer.

Do you believe it is possible to "forgive and forget"? Why or why not?

BECAUSE OF HIM

There is only one reason to forget the sorrow of yesterday— that sacred reason is because of Him. There is only one cause strong enough to pull you out of the past and into the possibility of hope— that cause is Him. There is only one explanation for choosing promise over disappointment—the explanation is Him.

Would you read this passage from Isaiah with me today? I pray you will savor every word as you delight in what God has done for you. These verses will remind you of the reason why every day is a perfect day to forget what ties you to your sad or trouble-filled past. Remember the Holy Spirit wrote these words specifically for you:

> *Fear not, for you will not be put to shame; and do not feel humiliated, for you will not be disgraced; but you will forget the shame of your youth, and no longer remember the disgrace of your widowhood. For your husband is your Maker, whose name is the LORD of armies; and your Redeemer is the Holy One of Israel, who is called the God of all the earth.* —Isaiah 54:4–5

You have permission to forget your past mistakes, the sins of yesterday, and even abuse if it was part of your history. No matter how others have treated you, the Father is head over heels in love with you. He longs to take you into His comforting arms and remind you that you are His forever. Today is a wonderful day to forget the mismanagement and the failures of yesterday. Today is a perfect day to forget disappointments, anger, and devastating relationships. You can forget your shame because of who God is.

DOES GOD FORGET?

I have some questions about God's ability to forget and perhaps you do as well. Knowing that God is omniscient, I have often wondered if God is able to forget anything at all.

- Does He forget my prayer requests?
- Does He need constant reminders about who to help on any given day?
- Is it possible that God forgets my sins?
- And if God *does* forget my sins, should I forget the sins of others?

Scripture does answer these questions for us, I believe, in a clear and concise way. If you are concerned that the Father keeps a list of your past sins and is ready to bring them up at a moment's notice, be assured that is not the case.

> *I, I alone, am the one who wipes out your wrongdoings for My own sake, and I will not remember your sins.*   —Isaiah 43:25

It is impossible for God to remember your sins, and if *He* forgets this part of your past, so should you. When you bring up a past sin in a conversation with God, He will likely reply, "I have no recollection of that event."

> *I will forgive their wickedness, and I will never again remember their sins.*   —Hebrews 8:12 NLT

This is quite possibly the best news you have ever heard! God forgets! He forgets all the sins and failures of your past and covers them with His mercy. The Hebrew word for "remember" is *zakar* and is used in both verses above. It's not that your sins slipped God's mind and then suddenly something popped up in His memory. He chooses not to remember them. God intentionally decides not to call your sins to His mind any longer because of mercy. God does not have amnesia as it pertains to your past, but He deliberately chooses to forget. What a wonderful God we serve!

If God purposefully has decided to forget how we have betrayed Him, we can do the same for others. We can forget.

LIFE QUOTE

I think the secret to a happy life is a selective memory. Remember what you're most grateful for and quickly forget what you're not.   —Richard Paul Evans

VERSE OF THE DAY

Brothers and sisters, I do not regard myself as having taken hold of it yet; but one thing I do: forgetting what lies behind and reaching forward to what lies ahead, I press on toward the goal for the prize of the upward call of God in Christ Jesus.

—Philippians 3:13–14

MEANINGFUL MOMENT

Make a list of the people who have hurt you. Make a list of the ways you have failed the Father. Now take that list and destroy it. It is over. It is forgotten.

DAILY DECLARATION

"I declare today that I choose to forget the pain of my past. I also intentionally choose to forget the pain others have caused me."

11

REMEMBER

I love remembering. I love remembering days from long ago and far away. I love to remember conversations, details from specific events, and the sound of my children's laughter. I love recalling childhood friends, my teachers from elementary school, and the lyrics to hymns. I love remembering the alto part from every choral piece I have ever sung, Bible verses I memorized as a child, and gifts I have given to others. I love calling to mind books I have read over the years, the sound of the waves upon the sand, and the songs I listened to when I was a teenager.

I am so much better at remembering than I am at forgetting. Remembrance is among the finest of arts one can develop over time. Reminiscing selectively yet truthfully can create mental masterpieces that are at once breathtaking and cherished. I believe there is no grander way to build a life of glorious intention than to purposefully remember the fingerprint of God upon one's life.

- As I recall the good, the bad often disappears.
- As I remember the blessings, the lack fades away.
- As I think on the magnificence, the minutia vanishes.
- As I call to mind the simple goodness of days gone by, I am given hope for tomorrow.

While remembering the good may certainly be classified as a *lost art*, perhaps it is time for us to understand the power that will invade our lives when we simply take the time to trace the fingerprint of God on yesterday.

What is one of the greatest blessings of your life from your childhood years?

_____

_____

What is one of the greatest blessings of your life from your adult years?

_____

_____

YOU CAN COUNT ON GOD

The first time the word *remember* is used in Scripture, it is used in reference to God's choice to remember the covenant He made with His people after the flood:

> I have set My rainbow in the cloud, and it shall serve as a sign of a covenant between Me and the earth. It shall come about, when I make a cloud appear over the earth, that the rainbow will be seen in the cloud, and I will remember My covenant, which is between Me and you and every living creature of all flesh; and never again shall the water become a flood to destroy all flesh. When the rainbow is in the cloud, then I will look at it, to remember the everlasting covenant between God and every living creature of all flesh that is on the earth.   —Genesis 9:13–16

Over the years of my study of Scripture, I have found a marvelous concept that rabbis have used for thousands of years. It is known as "the Law of First Mention." This law teaches us that, in order to understand a particular word or doctrine, we must locate the first place in Scripture the word or doctrine is revealed and then study that passage. Theologians believe the Bible's first mention of a concept offers the simplest and clearest presentation; doctrines can be then fully developed upon that foundation. So to fully understand an important and complex theological concept, Bible students are advised to start with its *first mention.*

Genesis chapter 9 is the first place in Scripture where the word *remember* is used, and it serves as a stunning illustration of the first thing we should always remember: God made a promise to always remember the covenant He had made with His dear children. God set a rainbow in the sky to serve as a reminder to Him and to us that He is a God who remembers.

We should always remember that we serve a God who remembers.

ONLY GOD

Whenever I am discouraged or feel I have run out of answers, I remind myself to think about the goodness of God in my life over the years. Discouragement often shouts while remembrance whispers. It is vital to join not only my mind but also my heart in the joy that assertively recalling the faithfulness of God will bring into days of despondency and hopelessness. I must remind myself to remember what only God can do.

The day the ark of the covenant was brought into the house of the Lord was a day of joy and memorable celebration for the people of God. David was so excited that he danced before the Lord in the city streets. This was also the day that David appointed the family of Asaph to be worshippers in the house of the Lord. Let's eavesdrop on the first song that this appointed family sang on a day of worship and jubilation:

> *Give thanks to the LORD, call upon His name; make His deeds known among the peoples. Sing to Him, sing praises to Him; speak of all His wonders. Boast in His holy name; let the heart of those who seek the LORD be joyful. Seek the LORD and His strength; seek His face continually. Remember His wonderful deeds which He has done, His marvels and the judgments from His mouth, you descendants of Israel His servant, sons of Jacob, His chosen ones! He is the LORD our God; His judgments are*

in all the earth. Remember His covenant forever, the word which
He commanded to a thousand generations.

—1 Chronicles 16:8–15

This hymn, thousands of years old, reminds us in the twenty-first century to "*remember His wonderful deeds*" and "*remember His covenant forever.*" There is no power like the power of Scripture, which will enable us to focus our minds on God and to fill our hearts with everlasting joy. As we read verses such as these, we must apply them to our lives today.

Make a list of at least five wonderful deeds that have happened in your life due to the goodness of God.

1. _____

2. _____

3. _____

4. _____

5. _____

What does it mean to you to "remember His covenant forever"?

_____

_____

MY LIST OF REMEMBRANCE

When God sets a principle into motion, the enemy will invariably come against it with one of his own. While God wants us to remember His blessings and His promises, the enemy wants us to remember everything that went wrong in our lives. As God's children, we are encouraged to remember answered prayers, godly relationships, and the miracles we have experienced. However, the enemy reminds us daily of disappointment, heartache, and human pain.

We must partner with God and only remember that which *He* has done in the annals of our lives. I have long loved the following verses, written by David, who offers a powerful list of items that I should write upon the memory book of my heart:

> *Bless the LORD, my soul, and all that is within me, bless His holy name. Bless the LORD, my soul, and do not forget any of His benefits; who pardons all your guilt, who heals all your diseases; who redeems your life from the pit, who crowns you with favor and compassion; who satisfies your years with good things, so that your youth is renewed like the eagle.* —Psalm 103:1–5

Looking back over the years of your life and searching for the goodness of God just may be the most vibrant discipline you will ever set into motion. Remembering the faithfulness and power of God will release untold joy in your ordinary days.

LIFE QUOTE

Perhaps nothing helps us make the movement from our little selves to a larger world than remembering God in gratitude. Such a perspective puts God in view in all of life, not just in the moments we set aside for worship or spiritual disciplines. Not just in the moments when life seems easy.

—Henri Nouwen

VERSE OF THE DAY

When I remember You on my bed, I meditate on You in the night watches, for You have been my help, and in the shadow of Your wings I sing for joy. —Psalm 63:6–7

MEANINGFUL MOMENT

As you read over the lyrics to this old hymn that you may have heard in childhood, make a list of the extravagant blessings of your life.

> *Count your blessings, name them one by one;*
> *Count your blessings, see what God has done;*
> *Count your blessings, name them one by one;*
> *Count your many blessings, see what God has done.*[2]

DAILY DECLARATION

"Today I declare that every day I have breath in my lungs, I will remember the blessings of God upon my life."

---

2. Johnson Oatman Jr., "Count Your Blessings," 1897.

12

REST

What do you believe the loveliest word in the English language might be? Some might believe these words to be among the most precious and comeliest words we speak:

+ *Mother*

+ *Home*

+ *Love*

+ *Family*

I have long wondered if one of God's favorite words is *rest*. He bids us to come to Him in the middle of our busyness and lives filled with stress and then splash in the incomparable peace only rest will bring. As we rest in His presence, we lay our cares and concerns at His feet and leave them there.

+ We can rest because He cares.

+ We can rest because He is able.

+ We can rest because He is Lord.

+ We can rest because His love is unconditional and kind.

+ We can rest because we have been invited into His presence.

Rest is not simply an option, but it is a necessity on the pathway to living an abundant life. You will never live the life for which you were created unless you choose to embrace the rest that only happens in His presence. Rest is more than just taking a Sunday afternoon nap, although there is nothing wrong with that. Rest is a mental attitude; it is an emotional position and a spiritual sanctuary. Rest is an act of obedience because the Father knows you best and loves you most. He simply wants what is best for you. Rest will always be His best.

What does the word "rest" mean to you?

How do you rest? Be practical.

THE OMNIPOTENT RESTS

God is omnipotent; He is all powerful. He never grows weary or runs out of energy. God is never tired of taking care of you nor is He exhausted from listening to the prayer requests of millions. The Lord never suffers from fatigue nor do your constant demands drain Him. He never sleeps … and yet He rests. Isn't that amazing?

The first time *rest* is mentioned in the Bible is when God rested after the monumental and miraculous task of creating the entire world. After the Lord God designed orchids, hyenas, the Grand Canyon, and you, He rested.

> *Thus the heavens and the earth were finished, and all the host of them. And on the seventh day God ended his work which he had made; and he rested on the seventh day from all his work which he had made. And God blessed the seventh day, and sanctified it: because that in it he had rested from all his work which God created and made.* —Genesis 2:1–3 WEB

Father God is our example of how to live not only a sacred life but also an extraordinary life; if He rested, then we must rest also. We must follow His magnificent example and incorporate the discipline of rest into our daily decisions.

Why do you believe God rested after His work of creation?

_____

_____

Do you believe rest to be a spiritual position or a physical one? Why?

_____

_____

THE PLACE OF REST

There is only one place where complete rest takes place, and it is likely not upon your bed at night with your head laying upon the perfect pillow and your body wrapped in your favorite comforter. The only truly restful place is near to the heart of God. If you will live your life near His loving and kind heart, your soul will adhere to a perpetual and rejuvenating rest. There is simply no place like it, next to the heart of God. As you lay in the unforgettable solace of His arms, your soul will find relief, and your heart will begin to beat in rhythm with His heart. As you feel the breath of God upon your weary essence, you will lie in unabated peace, filled with sweet hope.

This place of resting in His arms is discovered when you take off the cloak of comparison, when you relinquish your right to success, and when you forget the disappointment of yesterday. You must choose to pause from the cares of human living and join in the position of sacred repose.

It is both possible and necessary to instruct your mind to think only of Him and not of your carping to-do list. Lay it down, my friend, and find renewed energy in the quietude.

Begin by resting upon His glorious promises, reminding yourself daily of what He can do for weary travelers.

+ "He gives strength to the weary" (Isaiah 40:29).

+ He heals the sick. (See Psalm 103:3.)

+ He encourages the discouraged. (See 2 Chronicles 15:7.)

+ He provides for all our needs *"according to His riches in glory"* (Philippians 4:19).

+ He *"causes all things to work together for good"* (Romans 8:28).

What is another promise found in Scripture that encourages you to stand in faith?

_____

_____

Why are the promises of God a safe place to find rest?

_____

_____

REST IN GRACE

Often, the numerous and glaring mistakes I have made deny me of peaceful rest in Christ. As I lie upon my bed at night, I recall the things I wish I would have said differently, the actions I neglected to accomplish, the times I heard God's voice and did not obey. In those moments of self-inflicted exertion, I have found the sweetest place to rest is in the grace of God. His love for me covers all of my shortcomings and in His forgiveness, I discover a balm of peace. Rest is not established upon my good intentions, nor is it denied due to my failures; rest is a treasure discovered as I cover myself in His matchless grace.

I am invited to God's pallet of peace when at last I lay my will down for His higher plans. I discover mercy when I repent for my sins and linger in His love. His grace covers me and warms me in the worst of human conditions. I am at rest under His grace.

What does it mean to you to "rest in His grace"?

_____

_____

LIFE QUOTE

You made us for Yourself, and our hearts are restless until they rest in You.   —Saint Augustine

VERSE OF THE DAY

*Come to Me, all who are weary and burdened, and I will give you rest. Take My yoke upon you and learn from Me, for I am gentle and humble in heart, and **you will find rest for your souls**. For My yoke is comfortable, and My burden is light.*
                                                   —Matthew 11:28–30

MEANINGFUL MOMENT

Intentionally choose to participate in a few disciplines that bring rest to your soul. It may be listening to worship music or praying for others. It may be going for a walk outside or simply sitting down and breathing quietly.

DAILY DECLARATION

"I declare today that I will rest in His presence, on His promises and in His grace."

13

WALK

O h, how I love to walk! I walk in the heat, in the rain, and in the frigid cold. I always walk outdoors rather than on an indoor track or a boring treadmill. Part of my absolute gladness in choosing to walk outside is that I am able to savor the creative genius of God and drink in His magnificent handiwork. I walk when I feel like it and when I don't. I walk when I feel young and chipper, and when the effects of arthritis, joint pain, and the weariness that accompanies over six decades of active living are winning in my body.

Over the years, walking in the glory of the great outdoors has become my counselor, my reason to get out of bed in the morning, and my refuge from the mundane. As I tramp the hills around my home, I listen to the Bible, to an interesting podcast, or to a riveting book. It's all part of my daily routine, and it has added years to my life and life to my years.

A few years ago, as I was reading Psalm 23, a verse spoke to me as if I had never seen it before. You must understand that this new revelation was nearly ludicrous because I have probably read this particular psalm at least ten times or more every year of my life.

He lets me lie down in green pastures; He leads me beside quiet waters. He restores my soul.   —Psalm 23:2–3

How wonderful to know that God encourages us to spend time in the wonder of nature for a restorative purpose. Our soul is restored as we drink in the magnificence and splendor of His handiwork.

If you are weary today, could you sit outside for a minute or two? Or perhaps you could take a walk and be on the lookout for something rare and beautiful. You will discover, as I have, that a stroll in the great outdoors can be a winning strategy in the battle against depression, worry, or despondency.

What do you do for exercise?

_____

_____

How does creation restore your soul?

_____

_____

A LONG WALK

God's people found themselves in a wilderness of their own choosing in the Old Testament book of Deuteronomy. Because they had grumbled and complained, a journey that should have lasted only eleven days had turned into an encampment of forty years.

> *It takes eleven days to travel from Horeb to Kadesh Barnea following the Mount Seir route. It was on the first day of the eleventh month of the fortieth year when Moses addressed the People of Israel, telling them everything GOD had commanded him concerning them.* —Deuteronomy 1:2–3 MSG

As I ponder the predicament the children of God found themselves in, I wonder how many times I have spent time in a wilderness of life because of my own choices.

- When we worry or choose fear rather than trust, we have embraced a wilderness mindset.
- When we choose not to forgive, we have entered a wilderness mindset.
- When we overspend, overeat, or overindulge, we walk into the wilderness.

♦ When our anger becomes rigid bitterness, we are surrounded by the wilderness.

God wants you to walk out of the wilderness today. The Lord's wonderful plan for all His children is to live in the land of promises, where His presence is the fullest and His name is honored.

> *Across the Jordan in the land of Moab, Moses began to explain this Law, saying, "The LORD our God spoke to us at Horeb, saying, 'You have stayed long enough at this mountain. Turn and set out on your journey, and go to the hill country of the Amorites, and to all their neighbors in the Arabah, in the hill country, in the lowland, in the Negev, by the seacoast, the land of the Canaanites, and Lebanon, as far as the great river, the river Euphrates. See, I have placed the land before you; go in and take possession of the land which the LORD swore to give to your fathers, to Abraham, to Isaac, and to Jacob, and their descendants after them.'"*   —Deuteronomy 1:5–8

As I read the words that Moses spoke to the wilderness-weary Israelites, my heart leaps within me knowing that God is speaking those same words to me today. My friend, you have stayed at the mountain of discouragement and weariness long enough. It is time for you to pack your bags of trust and walk into the land the Lord has chosen for you to live in.

Perhaps you feel you have gone absolutely nowhere in your journey with the Lord and have experienced defeat after defeat. The mountain of bitterness is no place for a believer in Christ to set up camp and then to build a life. The Lord has a life of blessing and grace for you. Will you choose to walk toward it today?

> *May the LORD, the God of your fathers increase you a thousand times more than you are, and bless you, just as He has promised you!*   —Deuteronomy 1:11

No one can choose to walk for you; you must choose to walk for yourself. You must resolve to put one foot in front of the other and walk toward the promises of the Father regardless of how you feel or what your circumstances may be.

+ If life is hard … walk ahead anyway.

+ If your health is deteriorating … walk ahead despite it.

+ If you have no friends … walk toward the embrace of the Father.

+ If you have no finances … be resolute and walk in His strength.

See, the LORD your God has placed the land before you; go up, take possession, just as the LORD, the God of your fathers, has spoken to you. Do not fear or be dismayed.

—Deuteronomy 1:21

Today is a perfect day to remove your overcoat of fear and to replace it with a garment of praise as you walk toward all that God has for you. While you walk, whistle a happy tune, or sing a lovely song with the birds who are cheering you on. Speak with the Father as you march toward the hope-filled future He has chosen just for you. I can assure you that when you walk toward the land of joy and peace, you will never walk alone.

But the path of the righteous is like the light of dawn that shines brighter and brighter until the full day. —Proverbs 4:18

LIFE QUOTE

My beloved friend, keep your hand in that of the Master, walk daily by His side, so that you may lead others into the realms of true happiness. —George Washington Carver

VERSE OF THE DAY

You shall walk entirely in the way which the LORD your God has commanded you, so that you may live and that it may be well for

you, and that you may prolong your days in the land which you
will possess.   —Deuteronomy 5:33

MEANINGFUL MOMENT

You guessed it: today is your day to go for a walk. Take a deep breath and walk for at least five minutes. Maybe tomorrow you could make it ten minutes. While you walk, talk to God.

DAILY DECLARATION

"I declare that today I will walk away from bitterness, worry, and discouragement and will walk toward a future of bright hope."

14

BELIEVE

It was a nail-biting, down-to-the-wire college basketball game. The small Christian university I attended was definitely the underdog playing one of college basketball's elite teams in the NCAA tournament. If we won, we would be in the *Elite Eight*, which was no small feat for an unimportant, unknown school such as ours. We were no match for universities such as Kansas, Kentucky, and Duke, but we were playing our hearts out.

As the clock ticked away the final minutes, it looked like we would certainly lose without a miracle of Red Sea proportions. The chaplain of our university and his assistant were sitting in the stands cheering, yelling, and praying. When we were down by 10 points with only a few minutes to go, our beloved chaplain, Brother Bob, looked at his assistant and said, "Well, let's go before the crowd leaves. We're not going to win this game."

Larry, Bob's assistant chaplain, looked incredulously at his friend, his mentor, and his boss. His piercing blue eyes gazed straight into Brother Bob's eyes, and he declared with youthful enthusiasm, "But, Bob, it's more fun to believe!"

And so, they stayed until the end of this mismatched game, believing and cheering. Our small, midwestern university experienced a miracle that day as we won in overtime and became a proud member of the Elite Eight.

Before you read any further in this chapter, write out your definition of the word "believe."

What are you believing for today?

_____

_____

Why do you think it is "more fun to believe"?

_____

_____

ONLY BELIEVE

One of the songs that is seared on my heart is a tune that was popular in church when I was a teenager. Lyrics hold power; the words to this song have changed the way I process difficulties, impossibilities, and challenges.

Only believe, only believe;
All things are possible, only believe.[3]

+ When someone I love turns their back on God, I sing this song to myself.

+ When met with an unexpected bill in the mail, these lyrics jump into my heart.

+ When faced with cancer, I sang this song in every doctor's office.

+ When a door slams shut in my face, I remind myself of this powerful melody.

Believing that all things in life will certainly *"work together for good"* (Romans 8:28) may not be the easiest choice, but it is certainly the healthiest and the holiest choice a Christian can make. After all, we are not called *doubters*; we are known as *believers*. Believing is not just what we do, it is who we are; it is our very identity.

---

3. Paul Rader, "Only Believe," 1921.

How wonderful to know that our loving Father does not require us to figure out every situation, but He only asks us to believe in His character, in His promises, and in His Word. Perhaps the decision to believe fully and completely in the goodness of God is the most important decision you will ever make in life.

While it is true that it is the most difficult to keep our belief in God at full throttle when our world has imploded, that is the very time when the power of believing has the capacity to change everything. We must believe in His unchanging character when our hearts have been broken and when the storm is raging. We must believe that He loves us when we have been rejected or are alone. We must believe that He is able when a mountain lies in front of us or when a Goliath comes running at us.

Is there a song that often comes to your mind when you are going through a challenging situation? What is it?

WE ALL BELIEVE IN SOMETHING

Belief is always based upon trust. You will only believe in the people and principles who have garnered your trust. If someone repeatedly lies to you or even exaggerates from time to time, it becomes problematic to believe what they say. However, when someone is committed to telling the truth and lives up to their word, it is easy to believe not only in their words but also in their character. This is precisely the reason we can believe in the Lord.

> *God is not a man, that He would lie, nor a son of man, that He would change His mind; has He said, and will He not do it? Or has He spoken, and will He not make it good?*
> —Numbers 23:19

People will let us down, but the Lord never will. Politicians twist the truth, but the Lord never will. Friends reject us, but the Lord never will. You can believe in the Lord because He is worthy of your trust and faith.

Some people believe in the power of positive thinking; however, positive thinking on its own is nothing more than humanism. If you replace your thoughts with the Word of God and His promises, that is the type of thinking that will refine your belief system and change your outcomes. There are also people who believe in the ultimate goodness of mankind, and while that is certainly an optimistic way of thinking, someone will eventually let you down, betray you, or even reject you. Your belief must be in the faithfulness of Christ, who will never leave you or forsake you.

All belief systems that are not based upon the authority of Scripture and the goodness of God will never stand the test of time. He alone is able to meet every need, to win every battle, and to right every wrong. He alone is able—and so I will believe.

Why have you chosen to believe in Jesus Christ?

What does it mean to you to believe in the Word of God?

BELIEVE WHAT YOU BELIEVE IN

One of the challenges that will forever loom over the canyon between fact and faith is this: *do you believe the God you believe in?* To say you believe *in* God is a powerful and wonderful statement, but do you *believe* Him? Every man and woman must face this conundrum of the soul and decide not only to believe in God but also to believe Him.

+ I believe His promises.

+ I believe His character.

+ I believe His Word.

+ I believe He rose from the dead.

+ I believe Jesus is the Son of the eternal God.

When we finally believe the Lord more than we even believe our own feelings, it will be a place of power and consummate trust. Our feelings might shout but our belief system must prevail regardless of the circumstances, mistreatment, or doubts. We believe in Jesus Christ, who is our rock and our fortress, not in the instability of our emotions.

When you are struggling to believe for a miracle, perhaps a good prayer to pray, found in Scripture, would be this one:

> *But Jesus said to him, "'If You can?' All things are possible for the one who believes." Immediately the boy's father cried out and said, "I do believe; help my unbelief!"*   —Mark 9:23–24

I can't believe for you, and you can't believe for me. We each formulate our own belief system based upon what we hold most dear and most trustworthy. When we love Christ completely and know that His love for us is unchangeable, our belief will be in Him implicitly. We may not always understand, but we will always believe.

And let me just assure you one more time … it really *is* more fun to believe!

LIFE QUOTE

It is of no use to say to men, "Let not your hearts be troubled," unless you finish the verse and say, "Believe in God, believe also in Christ."   —Alexander MacLaren

VERSE OF THE DAY

Do not let your heart be troubled; believe in God, believe also in Me.   —John 14:1

MEANINGFUL MOMENT

Ask three people what they believe in. As you hear their answers, ask the Lord to give you the opportunity to share with them what you believe in.

DAILY DECLARATION

"I declare that I believe in Jesus, the Son of God, the Savior of the world. I believe in God the Father and in His goodness and faithfulness. I believe in the power of the Holy Spirit."

15

BLESS

The word *bless* is a uniquely Christian word although it has been hijacked by our culture. All blessings originate in the heart of God the Father, and we are called, as His beloved children, to become just like Him.

There is no doubt about it—we were created to bless the Lord and to be a blessing to others.

+ If you doubt the reason for your existence, remind yourself daily you were created to bless the Lord and to be a blessing to others.

+ As you wrestle with identity, remind yourself daily you were created to bless the Lord and to be a blessing to others.

+ As you struggle for purpose and meaning in life, remind yourself daily that you were created to bless the Lord and to be a blessing to others.

The invitation to *bless the Lord* is one of the most amazing partnerships in all human history. While the Lord is not in need of our enthusiastic words or even of our God-honoring lifestyle, our lives are the richer for blessing Him in every way possible. The Father is complete in Himself and nothing we could ever say to Him or do for Him would make His existence more wonderful. However, when we do choose to bless the Lord, your life and my life are the ones that will become infinitely more remarkable.

There is yet one more way this word *bless* was meant to impact our existence. We are also called to be a blessing to others along life's journey. We are instructed by Scripture to bless others, to bless those who persecute us, and to be a blessing daily.

Name one practical way you can bless the Lord today.

What is one practical way you can bless someone else today?

THE BLESSING OF "BLESS"

The word *bless* as used in the New Testament is the Greek word *eulogeo*, and it is a compound word comprised of *eu* and *logos*. *Eu* means "to be well off, fare well, prosper; acting well." The second part of this word, *logos*, can mean "what someone has said, the sayings of God, what is declared, anything reported in speech."

When *eu* and *logos* are placed together and become the word *eulogeo*, it captures an exciting and vivid meaning: "to praise or celebrate with praises; to invoke blessings; to ask God's blessing on a thing; to cause to prosper, to make happy, to bestow blessings on."

Your life is a hymn of praise and blessing to God the Father. Every word that proceeds from your mouth should have as its focused purpose the delight of blessing God, the Creator of the universe. Your heart is a symphony orchestra tuned to the celebratory key of blessing the Lord. There are, quite honestly, few other reasons for you to be alive today than for that of blessing the Lord who made you, who forgave you, and who cares about you.

> *But as for us, we will bless the LORD from this time and forever.*
> *Praise the LORD!*   —Psalm 115:18

+ When you don't know what to do, bless the Lord.

+ When your heart is broken, bless the Lord.

+ When friends betray you, bless the Lord.

+ When a storm is raging, bless the Lord.
+ When you wonder who you are, bless the Lord.

There is no higher reason for living and breathing than for the express purpose of blessing the Lord in all His splendor and glory. Your job description and your chief occupation on the time side of eternity is to bless the Lord. We should spend the hours of our days with our mind set on Him and our mouths primed to praise Him. Never should we blame the Lord, but we should continually bless the Lord; never should we doubt the Lord, but we should at all times bless the Lord.

> *I will bless the* Lord *at all times; His praise shall continually be in my mouth.*   —Psalm 34:1

Why is it important for a believer in Christ to "bless the Lord at all times"?

_____

_____

BLESS OTHERS

The second invitation the word *bless* presents is the wonderful opportunity to bless others. God gave us a tongue for three specific purposes: praising the Lord, declaring the Word, and encouraging others. The primary functions of the muscle between our pearly whites are found in those three audible actions.

What joy will be delivered to your life when you take the time to say an encouraging word to someone who has been made in the image of God! You might believe the sole purpose of the tendered encouragement is to inspire the receiver, but the truth is the one who will be encouraged the most is the one who has chosen to be the encourager.

Everyone needs a pick-me-up; everyone is desperate for just one kind, personal word of refreshment. Words bring life … and they can bring death; every word that comes out of your mouth is meant to be a life-bringing word of sweet blessing and outrageous encouragement. What we must realize, however, is that while blessing a person might begin with a simple word of encouragement, it doesn't end there.

A blessing is a *God-word* declared over a person; it is a reminder that God is good, and He cares deeply about a person's life. A blessing is a phrase of biblical hope spoken over someone. It is not sufficient to say, "I like you. I think you are wonderful." Those encouraging words, as influential as they are, come short of an actual blessing.

A blessing might sound like this:

+ "You are amazing! You have been made in the image of God!"

+ "The joy of the Lord is all over your countenance!"

+ "I love being with you. You exude the peace that comes from the Lord."

+ "Did you know that God has good plans for your life?"

+ "You are loved so much by the One who made you."

In Israel, when greeting a person, you utter the word, "Shalom." The word *shalom* is much more than a word of encouragement for peace or even a simple *hello* or *goodbye*. *Shalom* contains within its six unadorned letters a prayer, a blessing, a pronounced desire, and even a sacred benediction. Into this one magnificent word, *shalom*, is crammed the full blessing of God. Therefore, the blessing of *shalom* means that we, as God's beloved children, have the bequeathed power of blessing others with the authority of God. As we bless others, we are speaking on God's behalf and upon His request. We are partnering with the God of the universe to voice His supernatural invocation upon those in our lives.

What a rich life we have been called to! We can usher the *shalom* of God into the storm-tossed hearts of others by the words we speak.

List a few "shalom phrases" that you can use in daily conversation to bless others:

1. _____

2. _____

3. _____

GOD BLESSES YOU

Not only are you called to bless the Father and bless those who are in your life, but the word *bless* is even more substantial and far-reaching than those two significant purposes. God, in His infinite goodness and eternal kindness, has chosen to bless you and all that you are.

When Abram was weary with the constraints of age and with the disappointing circumstances of his life, God reminded this aging man that the blessing of God was upon his life.

And I will make you into a great nation, and I will bless you, and make your name great; and you shall be a blessing; and I will bless those who bless you, and the one who curses you I will curse. And in you all the families of the earth will be blessed.
—Genesis 12:2–3

The very same God who blessed Abram thousands of years ago has His eyes upon your life and has chosen to bless you with His goodness and with His power. How wonderful to know that you serve a God of blessing!

How has God blessed you this week? Spend some time thanking Him for His blessing upon your life.

LIFE QUOTE

The greatest blessing in the whole world is being a blessing.
—Jack Hyles

VERSE OF THE DAY

The LORD will give strength to His people; the LORD will bless His people with peace.   —Psalm 29:11

MEANINGFUL MOMENT

Look for opportunities today to sincerely bless people with your words and with your actions. You will be the richer for it!

DAILY DECLARATION

"I declare today that I am called to be a blessing to others and to spend my life blessing the Lord. I will live my life in the constant awareness of God's blessing upon my life."

16

EMPATHIZE

In a world of divisive politics, cold opinions, and preferential clatter, what has happened to empathy? Our culture drags us toward inclusive thought patterns and oftentimes away from our faith but what has happened to empathy?

The word *empathize* succinctly means "to be able to understand how someone else feels." While I don't always share the emotional responses of others, empathy invites me to understand why they might feel a certain way. Empathy brings beauty and unity to human relationships that are sadly missing when we refuse to partner with someone in their pain.

Empathy is the chosen ability to understand and share the feelings of another. When I empathize, I intentionally choose to view life from the perspective of the one who is hurting. Empathy has the power to connect us to others and to reduce human conflict. Rather than seeing a person as an adversary or as someone weaker, we can miraculously view them as a fellow pilgrim who is worthy of our understanding and respect.

Empathetic behavior bids me to lay aside my own feelings and to immerse myself in the pain of others. Perhaps the most stirring reminder to live an empathetic life comes from the apostle Paul in the book of Romans:

> *Rejoice with those who rejoice, and weep with those who weep.*
> —Romans 12:15

Write out your definition of the word "empathize".

Is it hard or easy for you to empathize with someone else's pain? Why?

_____

_____

THE SAME BUT DIFFERENT

The words *sympathize* and *empathize* are closely aligned in meaning yet each applies to a different stance in our human emotions. *Empathize* is the response of a person who directly feels the emotional state of another and thus enters into their pain. When we *sympathize* with someone, we feel sorrow for their sake but don't experience their emotions in the same intuitive manner.

Sympathize and *empathize* share the same root Greek word, *pathos*, which means "suffering, feeling, or emotion." These two words both require astute emotional intelligence. However, when I choose to empathize with a person's feelings, that response leads to a profound sense of common emotions and therefore shared understanding.

Empathizing with a person in deep pain means, in essence, to take on this person's feelings as your own. There is a descriptive word in German known as *einfuhlung*, which can be translated as "feeling into something." When you or I choose to empathize with the discouragement or sorrow of someone, we are able to experience their emotions on a personal level.

Both the ability to *sympathize* and *empathize* emanate from a fervent longing to comfort someone in the middle of their distress. What begins as sympathy often evolves into empathy as you pray for and seek ways to serve the person who is dealing with emotional pain.

People with high levels of empathetic behavior are often referred to as *empaths* due to their innate ability to fully share the personal experience or point of view of another person in anguish. Empathy is more than a feeling of sorrow; it is as if the heartbreak is theirs alone to bear.

When Lazarus, one of Jesus's dearest earthly friends, died a sudden and early death, the Bible records that *"Jesus wept"* (John 11:35). Jesus, although He was God in the flesh, exhibited empathetic behavior for those who were grieving the loss of a loved one. Even while Jesus was weeping, He knew that in just a few moments, the power of God would triumphantly raise Lazarus from the dead. Yet still, Jesus took the time to allow the human grief become part of His earthly experience.

Write out your definition of the word "sympathize."

_____

_____

How are sympathy and empathy alike?

_____

_____

How are they different?

_____

_____

SPEAKING EMPATHETICALLY

Empathetic behavior is perhaps expressed most vividly through our heartfelt words. The power of an auditory response to a person whose soul has been crushed is immeasurable. Often, it is our words, spoken with gentleness and understanding, that can begin the healing process.

> *Like apples of gold in settings of silver, is a word spoken at the proper time.*   —Proverbs 25:11

I have also discovered that as I speak empathetic words, my own heart joins with the one who is grieving in a meaningful and expressive manner.

- "I remember what it was like to ache for a baby month after month. I remember what it was like to have a broken heart and empty arms. I am praying for you."

- "I remember the days when I was so deeply depressed, I couldn't get out of bed in the morning. I recall the loneliness of that black pit of depression. I am committed to helping you live and breathe again."

- "I know what it is like to have a child leave their faith. The pain is enormous. You are not alone. I am praying for you."

Vocalizing empathetic words is a learned or developed skill that trumps a cool and rational personality. It is vital to habitually practice empathetic speech even when you may not understand why someone is deeply upset. I have found that it helps to just be quiet and listen to the pain of another. I am a *fixer* by nature, but empathy invites me to listen calmly and attentively without offering obvious suggestions. As I give attention to their expressed pain, it begins to permeate my very soul, and I am filled with the compassion of God toward this heartbroken individual. If God hovers near to the brokenhearted, then so must I.

The LORD is near to the brokenhearted.   —Psalm 34:18

As I sit with the one who is in pain and listen with an attentive and caring heart, I can then hear the voice of the Father and have the capacity to respond with the words of heaven.

Other than speaking empathetically, what are some other ways you can show empathy to someone in pain?

_____

_____

CHANGE THE WORLD

I believe at the core of every man and every woman is the ardent longing to make a difference. We each quietly yet passionately desire to change our corner of the world during our tenure on planet Earth. When you or I empathize with someone in the ravages of grief, it is an appointed opportunity to invest in eternity.

+ Empathy perpetually offers the summons to just be kind.

+ Empathetic behavior lays the foundation upon which kindness is built and tenderness is celebrated.

+ Empathy requires us to go into a world of pain and to partake of someone else's grief and discouragement.

+ Empathy is choosing to put on the mourner's garments and to weep with those who are weeping uncontrollably.

Christ entered the pain of the human condition and simply sat there with us. Empathy softly but unceasingly beckons us to be like Jesus.

Be kind to one another, compassionate, forgiving each other, just as God in Christ also has forgiven you. —Ephesians 4:32

LIFE QUOTE

If you can learn a simple trick, Scout, you'll get along a lot better with all kinds of folks. You never really understand a person until you consider things from his point of view ... until you climb into his skin and walk around in it.

—Harper Lee, *To Kill a Mockingbird*

VERSE OF THE DAY

Blessed be the God and Father of our Lord Jesus Christ, the Father of mercies and God of all comfort, who comforts us in all our affliction so that we will be able to comfort those who are

in any affliction with the comfort with which we ourselves are
comforted by God. For just as the sufferings of Christ are ours in
abundance, so also our comfort is abundant through Christ.
                                              —2 Corinthians 1:3–5

MEANINGFUL MOMENT

Think of someone who is currently experiencing deep and relentless pain. Ask the Holy Spirit to help you feel what they are feeling. Now, how can you allow this feeling of empathy to encourage this hurting person in both practical and personal ways?

DAILY DECLARATION

"I declare today that I will pray to sincerely understand the pain of others. I will continuously endeavor to embrace their pain as my very own."

17

DISCIPLE

I'll always remember my final moments with each one of my five children before they left the safety of the family home to embark on their collegiate experience. I knew whatever I said to them in that tender and definitive moment, they would carry with them the rest of their lives.

Should I remind them to brush their teeth every morning? To spend their money wisely? To turn away from sin and toward righteousness?

In that emotion-charged moment that happened five times over the course of fourteen years, all I could gulp out between great heaving sobs with violent tears coursing down my cheeks was, "I love you! Read your Bible!"

I wonder if Jesus experienced some of the same emotions I did as He prepared to return to the grandeur of heaven from the oxygen of human-based living. I believe deeply within my soul that the Father had planned from the beginning of time what Jesus would say to His disciples as He ascended back to the right hand of God, His Father.

> Go, therefore, and make disciples of all the nations, baptizing them in the name of the Father and the Son and the Holy Spirit, teaching them to follow all that I commanded you; and behold, I am with you always, to the end of the age.
> —Matthew 28:19–20

The final and impactful words that Jesus spoke while on earth carried the command to make disciples. Becoming a Christian who disciples others is not an optional assignment, but it was spoken in the imperative by Jesus, whose entire life was focused on making disciples. These words, spoken by Jesus yet conceived in the heart of the Father, are known as the Great Commission. We have been commissioned to make our lives count for all of eternity as we lead others to Christ and as we disciple those who have just come to the faith.

Why is discipling others in the body of Christ such a vital part of our earthly assignment?

_____

_____

WHAT IT IS

Christian discipleship consists of becoming more like Jesus every day. In order for you to become one who disciples others, you first must become a disciple yourself. The first step on this journey of fulfilling the Great Commission is for you to become a vibrant demonstration of Christ and His unshakable kingdom. Hidden in the expectation of these final earthly words of Jesus is a personal requirement: *"Am I living the life of a disciple?"*

Living the life of a disciple includes, but is not limited to, these daily, life-giving habits:

- Reading the Word every day.

- Spending time in prayer.

- Being an enthusiastic worshipper.

- Attending church on a regular basis.

- Tithing your resources to the local church or other ministries.

- Serving in your local body of believers.

- Cultivating the fruits of the Holy Spirit in your life.

- Attending a Bible study where the Word of God is taught clearly.

- Sharing your faith with others who don't yet know Christ.

- Going on short-term mission trips or sending others.

- Dying to self and living for Christ.

If the above list is overwhelming to you, allow me to assure you that becoming a disciple of Christ is not a list of *dos and don'ts* or *rights and wrongs*. Becoming a wholehearted disciple of Jesus is a healthy and even exciting way to grow in your faith.

+ If your desire was to be an Olympic athlete, you would train diligently and zealously.

+ If your calling was to play the piano at Carnegie Hall, you would practice relentlessly and daily.

+ If you wanted to climb Mount Everest, you would put every waking hour into your preparation.

+ If you wanted to be a master gardener, you would study, weed, plant, and water without complaining.

If your overarching goal in life is to follow Christ and then disciple others, your commitment must be habitual, joyful, and never-ending. I have told myself often these exciting truths:

+ I don't *have* to read my Bible ... I *get* to read my Bible.

+ I don't *have* to go to church ... I *get* to go to church.

+ I don't *have* to tithe ... I *get* to tithe.

+ I don't *have* to worship the Lord ... I *get* to worship the Lord.

+ I don't *have* to pray ... I *get* to pray.

In the early morning hours, as you open the sacred pages of Scripture, with a steaming cup of coffee in your hand, I hope you will recall this invigorating quote from *The Rabbi's Heartbeat* by one of my favorite authors, Brennan Manning:

> When God comes streaming into our lives in the power of His Word, all He asks is that we be stunned and surprised, let our mouths hang open, and begin to breathe deeply.

The call to be a disciple is not for the faint of heart nor is it for those who contentedly splash in mediocrity. Instead, it is for everyone who declares, "I want to be like Jesus more than I want to be like me!"

He must increase, but I must decrease.   —John 3:30

List three to five people who have discipled you over the course of your Christian walk.

_____

_____

Have you ever thanked them for their role in your life?

_____

_____

DELIGHTFUL DISCIPLINE

Now that you are a disciple, it is time for you to disciple someone else who is desperate for more of Jesus. One of the most delightful opportunities we are given, as followers of Jesus Christ, is to channel the overflow of our vibrant Christian walk into changing the life of someone else.

If you have been a Christian for twenty-four hours, there is someone younger in the faith who needs to know what you have learned thus far. If you have been a Christian for decades and have served Christ wholeheartedly since childhood, you should be discipling others by teaching Sunday school, leading a small group, or by teaching a Bible study.

If you have recently come back to your faith after stumbling in your walk, once you are grounded in your faith, you should be leading other prodigals back to the heart of the Father. Even your past mistakes and the wisdom that is now yours can bring healing to others.

If you want to add the glad prospect of discipling others who are just beginning their faith walk, there is first one obvious prerequisite: you must be a godly, fruitful, wise Christian if you hope to beget godly, fruitful, wise Christians. You will never be able to teach others what you yourself have not already learned as you have walked through valleys, deserts, and storms. You don't need to be perfect; you just need to be committed.

Make a list of three to five younger Christians with whom you could spend time in a mentoring or discipleship role. Pray about how the Lord could use you in their lives.

IT'S NOT GENETICS

I was born into a family of blue-eyed blondes with a sharp intellect, music in their souls, and a propensity toward large noses. When you are born into the family of God, it is not genetics that causes you to become a wise, fruitful Christian but it is oversight by elder brothers and sisters who have already lived the life of a disciple. You will be shaped by those you spend time with.

An important question to ask yourself is this: "As younger Christians spend time with me, who will they become?"

My father always told me, "Show me your friends and I will show you your future." I believe this statement especially holds true in the arena of discipleship. We will become, to a great degree, like those with whom we spend a lot of time. What a delight to know that others might become more like Jesus simply because they experience Jesus in me!

LIFE QUOTE

A true disciple has reached the point in Christian experience where there is no turning back. Follow him or her for 24 hours of the day and night. You will find you can count on that person's faithfulness to Christ and his or her joyful abiding in the Word of God.   —A. W. Tozer

VERSE OF THE DAY

And He summoned the crowd together with His disciples, and said to them, "If anyone wants to come after Me, he must deny himself, take up his cross, and follow Me."   —Mark 8:34

MEANINGFUL MOMENT

Prayerfully consider a younger brother or sister in the faith with whom you could intentionally spend time for the express purpose of discipleship. Now, do it!

DAILY DECLARATION

"I declare that I will become a disciple of Christ and that as I grow in my faith, I will purposefully disciple others. It is the life for which I was created."

18

SERVE

I have a dear friend, Carolyn, who is only four feet, eleven inches tall, and has lived a vibrant life for nearly eight decades despite physical ailments. She has had ten surgeries on her feet, including the amputation of a toe to alleviate excruciating pain. Her hands are crippled due to tendons that are shrinking. Most nights, she is unable to sleep due to horrific back pain.

When I went to visit Carolyn in the sunny south last year during my bone-chilling winter, she paid for my plane ticket and had an unsweetened iced tea with lemon waiting for me in the car when she picked me up from the airport. She knows what I like!

On Monday, the first day of my visit to Carolyn's warm and peaceful home, a woman had been invited to spend the afternoon with us so we could speak life and hope into her dry and thirsty soul. This woman has lived a life of prostitution and drug addiction but has recently come to know Jesus as her Lord and Savior. We spent three glorious hours with this formerly broken woman who now had the joy of the Lord all over her weathered face, thanks in large part to Carolyn's discipleship.

On Tuesday afternoon at church, we met a woman who is spending the last years of her life in a wheelchair due to the double diagnosis of both Lou Gehrig's disease (amyotrophic lateral sclerosis) and multiple sclerosis. Carolyn and I spent two hours with this debilitated woman as we laughed together, sang the songs of our faith, and shared the Word of God.

On Wednesday, Carolyn helped her daughter prepare lunch for twenty women who were coming to a Bible study. During the hustle and bustle of the morning, Carolyn received a message from a blind woman who wanted to join us but didn't have a ride. Carolyn sweetly sped away to pick up this woman who was walking by faith and not by sight.

On Thursday, we drove nearly an hour to have lunch with a ninety-four-year-old woman who had just lost her husband, a World War II veteran. What delight we had as we talked about the goodness of God while sipping tea and enjoying pimento cheese sandwiches.

And finally, on Friday, the last day of my sunny visit, Carolyn took me shopping and showered me with a beautiful new wardrobe. She also shared the Lord with the saleswoman who had been waiting on us.

Carolyn has determined to live a life of heartfelt service and cheerful aid despite her age or physical ailments. She is great in the kingdom of God—all ninety-five pounds of her gray-haired, osteoporosis-riddled body! And truly, she is one of the most beautiful women I have ever met because she looks just like Jesus.

> For even the Son of Man did not come to be served, but to serve, and to give His life as a ransom for many.   —Mark 10:45

Who is the most amazing servant you know?

_____

_____

Take the time this week to encourage someone who is a true servant.

THE ASSIGNMENT

Servanthood is as much a lifestyle as it is an assignment; serving others is not just discovered in the doing but also in the *being*. As I serve those the Lord has given to me, I must not do it under compulsion or begrudgingly; I must do it with my whole heart and with deep joy.

The heart attitude discovered in humble service is perhaps more important than the job that is to be accomplished. As we choose to be willing and glad servants, our goal is not to impress the church, our family, or others. Instead, our goal is to be more like Jesus, to lay down our lives in unpretentious and sacrificial love.

The kingdom of Christ has been described as an upside-down kingdom. As Christians, we often live our lives with a holy contradiction.

+ In order to live, we must die.

+ In order to gain, we must give.

+ We empty ourselves to become full.

+ We are strong when we are weak.

The holy contradiction of Christianity is nowhere more vivid than in the call to servanthood. If we long to become great in the unshakable kingdom of God, we must put on the clothes of a servant and spend our lives promoting others.

Who have you been called to serve?

_____

_____

Is this assignment a difficult one or an easy one for you? Why?

_____

_____

LIVING FOR THE KING

In her book *Keep a Quiet Heart*, Elisabeth Elliot tells the story of visiting the Dohnavur Fellowship in India. Elisabeth was especially observant of the women who lived at this compound and how they served one another without complaint. The women of this fellowship took care of the little children, handicapped individuals, the sick, and the elderly. They never traveled away from the compound and had no entertainment or diversion. The women worked in extremely primitive conditions without running water or washing machines, with only wood-burning stoves for cooking.

In one of the buildings of the Dohnavur Fellowship, Elisabeth saw this posted text: "There they dwelt with the King for His work."

That's the secret of service, my friend. When we serve, we do it for Him. When we love the difficult, we do it with His unfailing love. When we lay down our own lives, He gives us His strength. And when we die to self, He gives us His joy. Who wouldn't want to live a life like that?

What is your definition of the word "serve"?

IT'S THE LITTLE THINGS

When I was a young mother, my house was usually a disaster, my meals were generally chicken nuggets and french fries, and there was always laundry to be folded.

One day, an older woman from the neighborhood stopped by, and I was mortified—absolutely mortified—at the condition of my too-small home. This wonderful woman was wrapped in love and filled with joy. She picked up the baby, wiped a toddler's nose, and began to help me fold laundry. After folding mountains of laundry, she then tackled the dishes in the kitchen sink, all the while singing and speaking kindly to me and the children.

The next week, this godly woman asked me to have lunch at her home. My husband Craig arranged to come home for lunch so I could have an hour or two with this remarkable woman. Her home was spotless, but it was comfortable and cozy. We laughed and talked while she told me stories of the years she had raised her own family of three rambunctious boys. I drank in her wisdom, her life experiences, and her joy.

At the end of the delightful luncheon, this warm, older woman took my hands in hers, looked into my eyes, and said, "Carol, you love your family so much. It's obvious in every word you speak and in the way you are training them. I just wanted to remind you that one way you can show your love to your children is by providing a clean home as well as healthy meals for them. I know it's not always easy but serving in practical ways is a great gift of love."

I've never forgotten her words or her stunning example of servanthood. I began to view doing laundry, preparing nutritious meals, and even loading the dishwasher as small acts of unconditional love.

During those years of changing diapers, making beds, and cleaning bathrooms, I also learned I was not just demonstrating love for my family but love for my Savior as well. As I continued to serve *the least of these*, I was also serving my Master.

> *Then He will answer them, "Truly I say to you, to the extent that you did not do it for one of **the least of these**, you did not do it for Me, either."* —Matthew 25:45

Who are "the least of these" in your life?

_____

_____

How can you serve "the least of these" with deep joy and heartfelt love?

_____

_____

LIFE QUOTE

Great occasions for serving God come seldom, but little ones surround us daily; and our Lord Himself has told us that "he that is faithful in that which is least is faithful also in much."   —Saint Francis de Sales

VERSE OF THE DAY

It is not this way among you, but whoever wants to become prominent among you shall be your servant, and whoever desires to be first among you shall be your slave; just as the Son of Man did not come to be served, but to serve, and to give His life as a ransom for many.   —Matthew 20:26–28

MEANINGFUL MOMENT

Who can you serve today? Where can you serve today? Allow servanthood to become a lifestyle of great joy and delight.

DAILY DECLARATION

"Today I declare that I will serve willingly, joyfully, and sacrificially every day of my life."

19
SURRENDER

I recall, as a little girl, the sweet delight of going on vacation with my family. We inevitably begged our parents to stay at a motel where there was a swimming pool. Being raised in the Northeast, we rarely had the opportunity to dive into chlorinated water, swim across the pool, or splash to our hearts' content.

The highlight of swimming in these pools was when my dad jumped in with us. He was strong and athletic—and in my eyes, he could do anything. I recall to this day the fun we had dipping and diving and doggy-paddling with Dad.

In total freedom, wearing a bright pink bathing suit, with my blonde braids plastered to my skin, I would jump from the side of the pool and cry, "Daddy! Catch me! Catch me, Daddy!" And he did. He was always there to catch me.

My heart soared with joy as the one person I trusted most fully was found dependable and strong. My dad—there was no one like him.

What was your relationship like with your earthly father? Was he trustworthy?

_____

_____

Who has been a trustworthy person in your life?

_____

_____

EVEN JESUS

There are times in life when absolutely nothing can be done to change a situation. In those moments, we must quietly trust our capable Father to take care of that which is out of our control. In those moments, we learn the absolute freedom and joy that comes in fully surrendering our lives into His wonderful care.

> For you have been called for this purpose, because Christ also suffered for you, leaving you an example, so that you would follow in His steps, **He who committed no sin, nor was any deceit found in His mouth**; and while being abusively insulted, He did not insult in return; while suffering, He did not threaten, but kept entrusting Himself to Him who judges righteously.
> —1 Peter 2:21–23

When Jesus was being persecuted, mistreated, and reviled, He made a powerful decision. At this awful moment in His earthly life, He "*kept entrusting Himself*" to His Father in heaven. The Greek word that is translated as "*kept entrusting*" is *paradidomi*. This compound Greek word means "to entrust, to hand over, to surrender, or to commit." Jesus intentionally chose not to become angry or to despair, but He turned His life over to His Father and surrendered Himself entirely to the goodness of God.

We are called to be like Jesus when life is excruciatingly difficult and when everything seems to be coming against us. The example of Jesus bids us to a life of absolute surrender and radical trust. When you are in over your head and when the world seems to be conspiring against you, the most powerful choice you can make is to cry out, "Daddy! Catch me, Daddy!"

And He will. Your heavenly Father will open His arms and catch you. He will also capture your emotions, heartache, and pain. You can surrender your life to His ultimate goodness.

List three attributes in the character of God that are trustworthy:

1. _____

2. _____

3. _____

What is your definition of the word "surrender"?

_____

_____

WHAT SHOULD I SURRENDER?

The Bible consistently instructs the children of God to surrender our hearts and minds to Him. It is a daily act of surrender that yields the most satisfying and peaceful results. We don't surrender as an act of frustration nor as a last-ditch effort to get our own way. We surrender because we trust Him. We surrender knowing that He really *"causes all things to work together for good"* (Romans 8:28). We surrender because all power has been given to Him. We surrender because we want what He desires for our lives more than we want our own will.

Surrender is a bold choice that instigates an inward heart realignment. After we surrender all we have and all that we are to Jesus, peace rushes in where once there was confusion and conflict. As we lift our hands in worship and cry out, "I surrender," hope replaces fear while contentment raises its cheerful head.

Some aspects of your life that you might consider surrendering to the Lord include:

+ Your reputation

+ Your family

+ Your job

+ Your career

+ Your finances

+ Your marital status

+ Your retirement

+ Your burdens

+ Your hopes and dreams

+ Your priorities

+ Your time

+ Your health

When you surrender something, it means you no longer own it; that which you have surrendered no longer belongs to you because you have fully and completely yielded it to the care of someone else. When you choose to surrender an aspect of your life to the King, it is not a boomerang agreement. You are not allowed to take back what you have surrendered; you have fully released your control and are assured that whatever you have relinquished is in capable hands.

Perhaps our ability to surrender to the Lord is, in fact, a litmus test of our trust in Him. If we don't trust Him and in His ultimate goodness and authority, then it will be very difficult to surrender anything to Him. However, when we have learned to trust Him through all of life's storms and can say with Jesus, "Not my will but Your will be done" (see Luke 22:42), then surrender will become a reflexive response to His amazing nature.

What do you need to surrender to the Lord today?

_____

_____

Write out a prayer and surrender this aspect of your life to Him.

_____

_____

LIFE QUOTE

It is wonderful what miracles God works in wills that are utterly surrendered to Him. He turns hard things into easy, and bitter things into sweet. It is not that He puts easy things in the place of the hard, but He actually changes the hard thing into an easy one.　　—Hannah Whitall Smith

VERSE OF THE DAY

I have been crucified with Christ; and it is no longer I who live, but Christ lives in me; and the life which I now live in the flesh I live by faith in the Son of God, who loved me and gave Himself up for me.　　　　　　　　　　—Galatians 2:20

MEANINGFUL MOMENT

Make it your goal not just to surrender one aspect of your life to the Lord but to learn to live a surrendered life in all your ways. It helps me to write down what I have surrendered so that I can remind myself it no longer belongs to me.

DAILY DECLARATION

"Today I declare that I am a surrendered Christian. All that I am and all that I have is His. I can trust Him because He is good."

20

HOPE

We are the people of hope—and we serve the God of all hope! What an amazing journey as we travel through dry valleys, climb steep mountains, press on through vicious storms, and follow rocky pathways. No matter where you are on your journey and regardless of what the traveling conditions might be, always remember that hope is your compass.

Hope points the way toward a brighter tomorrow; hope places a spring in your step and renews the song of joy in your heart. Hope is the anchor in every storm and the peace treaty in every battle. If there is still breath in your lungs, you can remain hopeful because of His great and unwavering goodness.

Hope is a door that miraculously opens for those who walk by faith and not by sight. Hope is the small bird that sings in the darkest night when everything else is silent. Hope confronts every trial with the irrepressible joy of the Lord.

While some people may mournfully advise, "Don't get your hopes up," I can shout to the contrary that the people of God *must* get their hopes up! We must live in a state of heightened hope and defiant faith. If I am going to be accused of something, let it be that I am a woman who hopes too much and fears too little.

When you don't know what to do, you can always choose hope. When your heart has been broken by people or by events, a big dose of hope might be just what the doctor ordered.

So be strong and courageous, all you who put your hope in the Lord! —Psalm 31:24 NLT

What is your definition of the word "hope"?

_____

_____

Based on your definition, who is the most hopeful person you know?

_____

_____

ONLY HOPE

There is an amazing story found in the Old Testament that just might stir up hope in your heart today.

Asa was king of Judah and had an army of valiant warriors when Zerah came against him with an army of a million men and three hundred chariots. The odds against Asa were enormous, and the country of Judah was sure to be obliterated. There was nothing Asa could do to prepare his troops for such a slaughter, and there were no allies for him to call upon for help.

> Then Asa called to the LORD his God and said, "LORD, there is no one besides You to help in the battle between the powerful and those who have no strength; help us, LORD our God, for we trust in You, and in Your name have come against this multitude. LORD, You are our God; do not let man prevail against You."
> —2 Chronicles 14:11

Asa reminded the Lord that he had no one to help him but the Lord. Only God could help Judah fight this battle.

In the classic devotional *Streams in the Desert*, the author quotes theologian F. B. Meyers:

> Put God between yourself and the foe. To Asa's faith, Jehovah seemed to stand between the might of Zerah and himself, as one who had no strength. Nor was he mistaken.

We are told that the Ethiopians were destroyed before the Lord and before His host, as though celestial combatants flung themselves against the foe in Israel's behalf, and put the large host to rout, so that Israel had only to follow up and gather the spoil. Our God is Jehovah of hosts, who can summon unexpected reinforcements at any moment to aid His people. Believe that He is there between you and your difficulty, and what baffles you will flee before Him, as clouds before the gale.[4]

My definition of the word *hope* is to "put God between myself and the foe." I can do that; can you?

MY FAVORITE

I love the Word of God more than I love chocolate, oxygen to breathe, or even spending time with my amazing adult children. I would rather read the Bible than go shopping, enjoy a day at the beach, or live in my dream home. As you can imagine, after being a student of the Bible for most of my adult life, there are many passages in Scripture that have sprung to vibrant life in my heart. Whenever I meditate on one of these precious verses or teach on these treasured Scriptures, I inevitably proclaim, "This is one of my favorite passages in all of Scripture." And the truth is, it's all my favorite. I love every verse, every word, every book in the irreplaceable Word of God.

One of my favorite Scriptures that never ceases to make me smile and gives me a hope not tied to my earthly circumstances is found in the book of Romans written by the apostle Paul:

> *Now may the God of hope fill you with all joy and peace in believing, so that you will abound in hope by the power of the Holy Spirit.*   —Romans 15:13

The words penned by Paul and inspired by the Holy Spirit ricochet through the centuries and find fertile soil in the hearts of all

---

4. Mrs. Charles E. Cowman, *Streams in the Desert* (Los Angeles: Oriental Missionary Society, 1943), 6.

who live today in the twenty-first century. Paul's words are at once a prayer, an admonition, and a heartfelt desire. He soberly realized the early church would never make it through the tribulations they would soon face without the hope that only God can give. And so, he told them, "Church … get your hopes up!"

Hope never enters a hurting heart alone but invariably brings its twin sister, *joy*, and its little brother, *peace*. Hope also understands that first believing in the God of hope will ultimately and quickly reproduce hope in the soul of a discouraged Christian. Hope was never meant to stay the same size; when the Father stirs up your hope, it multiplies exponentially until it bursts out of your heart unto others.

As you stir up your belief in the goodness of God and as you open the door of your heart to the family of hope, a miracle occurs. Where once there was discouragement and despair, you are now absolutely dripping with hope. You are up to your ears in hope, and it is gleefully threatening to swallow you alive!

The Holy Spirit loves to barge into the life of a disheartened believer and to unashamedly shout, "It's time to get your hopes up! God is still on the throne! He has never lost a battle yet!"

Hope will enable you to endure what others can't endure and to sing while the arrows are flying around you. When hope and the Holy Spirit take charge of the battleground of your heart, a sacred celebration is about to begin and you, my friend, are the guest of honor.

What is one of your favorite passages of Scripture? Write it out below.

WHY HOPE?

Hope is a choice that begins in one's mind and then travels to the heart. While you might not always *feel* like hoping, if you can intentionally *choose* to hope, the feeling will certainly follow.

Jeremiah is remembered as *the weeping prophet* because his grief over the state of the world was pervasive. Jeremiah wept because the people of his generation had rejected God and were living lives of self-ishness and sin. This sad prophet wrote the book of Lamentations, which is known as *the book of tears*. In many ways, this short book tucked into the Old Testament is a funeral dirge written for the fallen city of Jerusalem.

In the middle of Jeremiah's wretched pain, he suddenly reminds himself who God is and why there is always a reason to hope:

> *Yet I still dare to hope when I remember this: the faithful love of the* Lord *never ends! His mercies never cease. Great is his faith-fulness; his mercies begin afresh each morning. I say to myself, "The* Lord *is my inheritance; therefore, I will hope in him!"*
>
> —Lamentations 3:21–24 NLT

Isn't this astounding? Don't you just want to stand and cheer for Jeremiah? Isn't your heart just about to burst out of your chest? Jeremiah's declaration of joy and hope is only possible because he removed his focus from his disappointment and placed it on the faithfulness of God.

Hope will only be possible for you, my friend, when you listen to Jeremiah and imitate his behavior. Call to mind the Lord's loving-kindness in your life and remind yourself that His compassion extends to you. The Father has not forgotten you; indeed, His faith-fulness is the foundation of your life. You can hope because you have Jesus.

A PRISONER OF HOPE

Many of us are prisoners without realizing it. A prison is a dis-couraging and limiting place to live. Perhaps you realize that you have been a willing prisoner at one of these emotional penitentiaries:

+ A prison of negativity and criticism
+ A prison of unhealthy mental habits

- A prison of anxiety and fear
- A prison of former abuse and past pain
- A prison of regret and failure
- A prison of wasting time on things that don't actually matter
- A prison of comparison

If you are going to be a prisoner of anything at all, let it be a prisoner of hope. Choose to be in bondage to *hope*, a magnificent cellmate of the very best kind.

What has been the prison of your own making?

_____

_____

How can you get out of the prison you've been living in and change addresses to the prison of hope?

_____

_____

At the end of my life, as I look back over the years I have lived and the things that I valued, I pray that I can declare over my life, "Well, at least I had hope!"

While it is true that your future is unknown and you are unsure what lies ahead, remind yourself often that God holds all the tomorrows of your life, and He has promised never to leave you or forsake you. Tether yourself to the promises of God and live in the prison of hope. God has a reward for those who choose to live in their lives in the stronghold of hope; He intends to give you a double blessing of unmatched strength. Hope always produces a double blessing.

Return to the stronghold, you prisoners who have the hope; this very day I am declaring that I will restore double to you.
                                                                —Zechariah 9:12

LIFE QUOTE

Hope is the thing with feathers that perches in the soul, and sings the tune without the words, and never stops at all.

—Emily Dickinson

VERSE OF THE DAY

But I will hope continually, and will yet praise thee more and more. —Psalm 71:14 WEB

MEANINGFUL MOMENT

What situation in life has stolen your hope from you? It's time for you to tie yourself to hope and to trust the Lord! What is one practical and hopeful habit you can cultivate?

DAILY DECLARATION

"I declare from this day forward, I will be a prisoner of hope. I will get my hopes up and I will welcome hope, joy, and peace into my life in Jesus's name."

21

ENJOY

Perhaps genuine enjoyment is one of the most overlooked rhythms of a committed Christian life. We falsely believe that denying ourselves all sorts of simple pleasures is somehow a more sacred, holy way to live. The truth is we bring pleasure to the Father's heart when we bask in the wonder of all that He has generously given to us. Enjoying life is not a sin, but it just may be a vital aspect of the Father's strategy to help us stay afloat in a sea of difficulties and challenges.

When we are enjoying the right things, our lives will reflect a purposeful sparkle and a contented glow. When we prioritize enjoying the wrong things, we will discover, as Solomon did, that this type of enjoyment is mere futility. (See Ecclesiastes 2:1–11.) Possibly the true dilemma is not whether we should live a life of enjoyment but exactly what is ours to enjoy.

The word *enjoy* means to take delight, satisfaction, or pleasure; it can also mean to possess or to benefit from. There are certain activities and experiences in life that are given to us for sheer delight and sheer pleasure. There are also relationships and opportunities from which we benefit in a meaningful and impressive way. As we realize that every good gift is from above, we are then able to fully enjoy the life that is ours.

> *Every good thing given and every perfect gift is from above, coming down from the Father of lights, with whom there is no variation or shifting shadow.* —James 1:17

What does it mean to you personally to truly enjoy the life you have been given?

_____

_____

NOT FOR ME

The world's way has never been God's way, and we must wisely choose for ourselves what God has given to us to enjoy. The world has concocted a false narrative on how to enjoy the years we have been given. Perhaps you have heard some of these twisted philosophies coming from our culture:

+ You only live once!
+ If it feels good, do it!
+ Live your best life!
+ Live your own truth!
+ Do what makes you happy.
+ You get to say everything you think, feel, and believe.
+ You are enough!

The deception in all of those life philosophies is that the focus is on self-importance, self-satisfaction, and self-entitlement. But the only way to truly enjoy life is to incorporate God into every moment, every decision, every relationship, and every thought.

Can you think of other phrases the world asserts in our quest to live an enjoyable life?

_____

_____

TRUE ENJOYMENT

There is only one way to thoroughly enjoy the life you have been given and that is by recognizing who God is and by hiding your life in His promises. As you pursue the Lord and all He is, you will discover a rare and treasured enjoyment that formerly was nowhere to be found.

Let's eavesdrop on a conversation that Moses was having with the children of Israel one significant day. As Moses spoke with them concerning their priorities and their life choices, he also reminded them what it takes to live a life of complete enjoyment and well-being:

> So remember this and keep it firmly in mind: The LORD is God both in heaven and on earth, and there is no other. If you obey all the decrees and commands I am giving you today, all will be well with you and your children. I am giving you these instructions so you will enjoy a long life in the land the LORD your God is giving you for all time.   —Deuteronomy 4:39–40 NLT

My friend, the advice of Moses rushes through millennia and lands a bullseye in our lives today. For us, as the children of God in the twenty-first century, to live a life of godly enjoyment and pleasure, the guidelines are the same:

+ Recognize the lordship of God the Father and Jesus the Son.
+ Obey the Word of God

Genuine enjoyment is a result of placing the Lord on the throne of our hearts and agreeing with His Word. Quite frankly, you don't have a better idea than God and neither do I.

What is one of your favorite memories that you love to retell?

_____

_____

Why do you think that memory brings you joy?

_____

_____

WISDOM

The great King Solomon struggled with how to truly enjoy the life that was uniquely his. Solomon lived a magnificent life and was known as the wisest man to ever live ... and yet he still wrestled with what he was allowed by his Creator to enjoy. Solomon had been given riches, honor, and fame, and yet he pronounced it all as vanity or futility. The book of Ecclesiastes, written by this memorable king, reminds us to find our fulfillment and to seek happiness in God alone. God is the only one who can give life meaning; He is the only one who can help us discover eternal enjoyment. Solomon clearly states that temporary delight must bow to the riches of eternity.

> *So I decided there is nothing better than to enjoy food and drink and to find satisfaction in work. Then I realized that these plea-sures are from the hand of God. For who can eat or enjoy any-thing apart from him?* —Ecclesiastes 2:24–25 NLT

King Solomon reiterated these same thoughts as he continued to search for meaning in the ordinary days of his magnificent life:

> *Even so, I have noticed one thing, at least, that is good. It is good for people to eat, drink, and **enjoy** their work under the sun during the short life God has given them, and to accept their lot in life. And it is a good thing to receive wealth from God and the good health to enjoy it. To enjoy your work and accept your lot in life—this is indeed a gift from God.*
> —Ecclesiastes 5:18–19 NLT

I don't know what type of happiness you are searching for today, and although I am not nearly as wise as King Solomon, I can assure you that there is no life, happiness, or enjoyment apart from knowing Christ and cultivating a heart of gratitude for what He has given.

EXTRAORDINARY ENJOYMENT

Are you ready for an extraordinary verse? Are you prepared to linger in the delight of discovering God's will?

Instruct those who are rich in this present world not to be conceited or to set their hope on the uncertainty of riches, but on God, who richly supplies us with all things to enjoy.
—1 Timothy 6:17

God richly supplies us with everything to enjoy! Isn't that amazing? What have you been given by the Father that you might be ignoring? What are some of the sweet gifts that are yours simply because the Father loves you and desires for you to live a life of enjoyment?

+ The birds that sing outside your window every morning.
+ The laughter of the children in your neighborhood.
+ The friendly girl at the grocery store.
+ A car that runs smoothly and takes you where you need to go.
+ A roof over your head and a pillow under your head.
+ A steaming cup of coffee in the early morning hours.
+ Your Bible.
+ A dear friend who encourages you along life's way.
+ The great hymns of the faith.
+ A juicy piece of watermelon on a hot summer day.
+ The glory of the sunset in the western sky.
+ The flowers in the village park.
+ A sunrise every morning and a sunset at night.

Life is too short not to enjoy the people, events, and moments that God gives to us every day. My mission in life is to wring the joy out of an ordinary day and to look for the fingerprint of God with every breath I take. That, my friend, is enjoying life at its finest!

Make a list of some of the things that you enjoy about an ordinary day:

1. _____

2. _____

3. _____

4. _____

5. _____

LIFE QUOTE

But if you possess faith, your heart cannot do otherwise than laugh for joy in God, and grow free, confident, and courageous. For how can the heart remain sorrowful and dejected when it entertains no doubt of God's kindness to it, and of his attitude as a good friend with whom it may unreservedly and freely enjoy all things?   —Martin Luther

VERSE OF THE DAY

You will make known to me the way of life; in Your presence is fullness of joy; in Your right hand there are pleasures forever.
                —Psalm 16:11

MEANINGFUL MOMENT

Spend the hours of today intentionally looking for things to enjoy. At the end of the day, make a list of gratitude for the things you discovered.

DAILY DECLARATION

"I declare that today I will enjoy my life. I will smile at children and sing the songs of faith. I will forgive others, and I will encourage people in my pathway. This is the day the Lord has made! I will rejoice and be glad in it!"

22

GIVE

If you have struggled with your purpose in life, my friend, struggle no longer. If you have always wondered why you were born and what God had planned for your life, the wondering will cease today. The answer is as obvious as the heart that beats within you and the world that is around you.

You were created to be an outrageously generous, perpetually benevolent, always open-handed giver! It's why you were born! You were created to be the most unselfish giver at this moment in history.

> *Each one must do just as he has decided in his heart, not reluctantly or under compulsion, for God loves a cheerful giver. And God is able to make all grace overflow to you, so that, always having all sufficiency in everything, you may have an abundance for every good deed.* —2 Corinthians 9:7–8

Will you fulfill your destiny? Will you give and give and give again? Will you allow the Lord to change the world around you through your lavish generosity? No one can fulfill your destiny as well as you can, and there is no better time than today to begin living in your extraordinary destiny.

Why do you believe that being a generous giver is part of God's plan for your life?

_____

_____

What's the difference between tithing and giving?

_____

_____

THREE IMPOSSIBILITIES

You may or may not believe it, but there are at least three things in life that are truly impossible. Would you like to know what they are?

+ It's impossible to out-dream the Lord.

+ It's impossible to out-love the Lord.

+ It's impossible to out-give the Lord.

Regardless of how generous you are, you will never be able to give more to others or to the Lord than has already been given to you by His generous hand. As you plant your seeds of pure-hearted generosity into the fertile soil of the kingdom of God, an amazing harvest will spring up out of the formerly barren ground.

Generosity is the family business, and our Father has called us to join Him in giving our resources, our time, and our talents to others in need.

Can you think of an impossibility other than the three that I've listed?

_____

_____

ONE GENEROUS WOMAN

Jesus had spent the day being questioned by the religious leaders and He had been teaching parables to those who were listening. He was likely tired after the intense day and decided to sit down opposite the treasury in the temple. As He sat there, He observed the people whom He loved so dearly.

And Jesus sat down opposite the treasury, and began watching how the people were putting money into the treasury; and many rich people were putting in large amounts. —Mark 12:41

I can picture Jesus, sitting quietly to the side, watching people come and go and considering their giving habits.

Isn't it wonderful to know that Jesus still watches us today? His eyes are always on His children, and He is perpetually looking into our hearts as we go about our daily lives.

Tradition teaches that the wealthy in the first century made a great show of giving. They dressed in beautiful robes made especially for the occasion of bringing large sums of money to the temple. Their robes were fashioned from brilliant colors; I can't help but wonder if they resembled pretentious peacocks strutting around, impressed by their own importance. Attached to their garments were gold tassels that bespoke of unmatched wealth and fortune. These affluent benefactors reeked of prosperity and position.

The opulent members of society did not stoop to carry their own money into the temple but had servants who walked behind them carrying coffers made of gold, silver, and jewels. The servants were forced to carry these expensive, bulky containers high over their heads so everyone in the temple was aware of the magnificence of the gift.

The servants were expected to pour the extravagant amount of money from high above their heads into the metal containers positioned to receive the overflowing offering. The sound was enormous as the coins crashed and clanged into the receptacles. The echoing reverberated through the cavernous halls of the temple.

The rich and famous of Jerusalem were impressed by their own pompous giving and at the noise their very presence made. It was the roar of pride, not of generosity.

And still Jesus sat there quietly. He was not impressed by the earthly show of bombastic arrogance. I wonder if He was sad—if perhaps a tear or two ran down His sun-weathered cheeks.

It was the week before Passover, also known as paschal week. The temple was crowded with people who attended just for the sake of tradition and for show.

On the other hand, the poor came in quietly, trying not to draw attention to their humble condition. These impoverished members of society walked in almost ashamedly, without a parade and without undue noise.

> *Then a poor widow came and dropped in two small coins.*
> —Mark 12:42 NLT

A poverty-stricken widow arrived that day as Jesus was watching, and she dropped in two small copper coins. Ping. Ping. There was no echo and no clang when her gift was given. Just ping. Ping.

The indigent widow didn't wear brightly colored robes but the garb of those who grieve. She had no servants, no high-held containers, just her sweaty, wrinkled hand. Ping. Ping.

> *God does not see as man sees, since man looks at the outward appearance, but the LORD looks at the heart.* —1 Samuel 16:7

Jesus saw the heart of this amazing woman and knew she was fulfilling her purpose in life. She had come to give all she possessed to the Father's house and to His people out of pure love.

Although Jesus had been teaching all day, He used this moment to teach yet another lesson to His band of brothers.

> *Calling His disciples to Him, He said to them, "Truly I say to you, this poor widow put in more than all the contributors to the treasury; for they all put in out of their surplus, but she, out of her poverty, put in all she owned, all she had to live on."*
> —Mark 12:43–44

Write this on your hearts, my friends. It is easy to give out of our surplus but this widow who lived two thousand years ago gave everything she had to the work of God. We don't know her name but we know her heart.

There was no greater life of poverty in that ancient culture than that of a widow. She didn't receive a monthly Social Security check,

and there were no life insurance policies of which she was the benefi-
ciary. She likely had no consistent income and yet she gave everything
she had out of pure love for the Father and for His people. Perhaps
my depth of love for the Lord is measured by how much I give to Him.

The astounding lesson from this one lonely woman's life is that
we must hold our possessions and our resources with an open hand
rather than with a closed fist. We must give our money, our time, our
words of encouragement, our acts of service, and our resources even
when we feel we have nothing left to give.

Jesus viewed the widow's gift as more significant than all of the
contributions of the enormously wealthy combined. Jesus refuses to
assess people's lives in the same manner that our culture does. Always
remember that God looks at our hearts.

You must never think that the little you have to offer in terms
of time, money, or possessions won't make a difference. Little really
does become much when you place it in the Master's hands of
multiplication.

What have you learned from this story?

THE MORAL OF THE STORY

The amount you give is not nearly as important as what you have
left after you give to the Father and to His work. The destitute widow
gave all she had; she had nothing left after her generous contribution.

Giving is not the exclusive privilege of the rich; paupers are called
to be an energetic source of provision for the cause of Christ as well.
God always provides for givers.

+ If you want to prosper in life, learn how to be a generous giver.
+ If you concentrate on being a blessing, God's blessing on your
  life will be immeasurable.

♦ When you give, you are storing up God's goodness and favor to your account.

How can you give to others in ways that are not financial?

_____

_____

LIFE QUOTE

God has a way of giving by the cartloads to those who give away by shovelfuls.   —Charles Spurgeon

VERSE OF THE DAY

Give, and it will be given to you. They will pour into your lap a good measure—pressed down, shaken together, and running over. For by your standard of measure it will be measured to you in return.   —Luke 6:38

MEANINGFUL MOMENT

Evaluate your financial giving by looking at your banking records for the past year. Evaluate the giving of your time by looking at your calendar for the past year.

DAILY DECLARATION

"I declare that I know my purpose. I am called to be a giver. I will be generous with my time, talents, and resources."

23

HINENI

I assume you must be scratching your head right now and wondering, "What in the world does *hineni* mean? I have never seen that verb!"

Allow me to reassure you that you have just met your new, favorite verb, *hineni*, pronounced hee-nay-nee. Although it is not an English word but a Hebrew verb, its meaning is so vast and compelling I knew it must be included in our riveting list of exacting, exciting verbs.

Once you understand its meaning, *hineni* is the verb you will use over and over again in your response to the voice of the Lord in your life.

What has been your favorite verb we have studied together so far?

_____

_____

How are you applying this verb to your life?

_____

_____

I WILL GO

Joseph has always been my favorite Old Testament character. He was young, handsome, and godly. When his life fell apart at the hands of his ten older brothers, he continued to serve the Lord wholeheartedly and his testimony was one of impeccable excellence. Honestly, what's *not* to love about a young man like that?

Joseph had been the object of his brothers' ridicule and scorn during his teenage years. The Bible offers this detail about the animosity in his brothers' hearts toward Joseph:

> *His brothers saw that their father loved him more than all his brothers; and so they hated him and could not speak to him on friendly terms.*   —Genesis 37:4

While Joseph was at home with his father, his older brothers had been sent to pasture their father's flock in Shechem. And his father, Israel, "*said to Joseph, 'Are your brothers not pasturing the flock in Shechem? Come, and I will send you to them.' And he said to him, 'I will go'*" (Genesis 37:13).

Joseph was sent by his father, Israel, also known as Jacob, to see if all was well with his older brothers who were shepherding the family flock somewhere near Shechem. This was a difficult request that Israel was making of Joseph, knowing how his older sons had treated him in the past.

One detail of this passage so dear to my heart is Joseph's immediate response to his father's request. Joseph wholeheartedly replied, "I will go."

"I will go" is the amazing and life-changing Hebrew word, *hineni*. The literal translation of this phrase from the Hebrew *hineni* is, "Here I am."

Joseph was telling his beloved father, "Dad, I am at your service. Whatever you ask of me, I will do. Wherever you send me, I will go."

Some Bible scholars translate this phrase as, "I am ready."

READ IT PERSONALLY

I have discovered eternal impact when I choose to read a passage personally and thereby apply its theme to my own life. As we ponder this passage from the Old Testament, we must search our hearts and remember how we have replied to our heavenly Father when He has asked something difficult of us.

Are you ready, like Joseph, to go wherever the Father sends you?

- When the Lord asks us to work in the church nursery or teach Sunday school, we must respond, "I will go."
- When the Lord asks us to be kind to a difficult person, we must respond, "Yes, Lord."
- When the Lord requests that we give money to a missionary, a person, or a ministry, we must respond, "I will do it."
- When the Lord lays it on our heart to be a foster parent, our instant response should be, "I am ready."

What difficult assignment has the Lord given to you lately?

_____

_____

How have you responded?

_____

_____

As you look back over the years of your life, do you wish you had said, "Hineni" rather than "Not me," to the Lord?

_____

_____

FAITH FOR THE MOMENT

There are other faith heroes in the Bible who also responded with this massive, enthusiastic, and yet humble word when asked to do something difficult for the Lord.

Abraham responded, "Hineni" when God asked him to sacrifice his son, Isaac, on the altar. (See Genesis 22:1.)

Moses declared, "Hineni" when he stood in front of a burning bush and was required to lay aside his insecurities for the greater plan of God. (See Exodus 3:4.)

Isaiah responded quickly in obedience when he heard God's call.

Then I heard the voice of the Lord, saying, "Whom shall I send, and who will go for Us?" Then I said, "Here am I. Send me!"
—Isaiah 6:8

"Hineni" is a declaration of unconditional and vested availability, of complete readiness to serve. When we are brave enough to respond with "hineni" to whatever God asks of us, it is an answer birthed in deep faith.

I am completely undone as I realize that Abraham, Moses, Isaiah, and Joseph did not know what God was asking of them and yet they still responded, "Hineni."

The wonder of it all is that God, our Creator and Father, has also said, "Hineni" to His beloved children.

Then you will call, and the LORD *will answer; you will cry for help, and He will say, "Here I am."*   —Isaiah 58:9

Who do you know today who has responded with a fervent "hineni" to a challenge in life?

MY HEROINE

Several years ago, at a Christian writers' conference, I met an amazing woman of God with whom I had an instant heart connection. Her name was Lucinda Secrest McDowell, affectionately known as "Cindy" to her family and close friends.

We stayed in touch through email, texting, and phone calls through the next decade and loved being together whenever our paths crossed. Honestly, in true Cindy fashion, she was much better at staying in touch than I was, but I loved her dearly.

Cindy had lived with Elisabeth Elliot when she was a graduate student at Gordon Seminary and as part of her daily duties had transcribed Jim Elliot's journals. Cindy knew how much I loved Elisabeth and sent me an autographed copy of one of her early books that was no longer in print. I treasure this undeserved gift—but I treasured Cindy's heart most of all.

Cindy was a sterling writer and had a heart of pure gold; she was intent on sharing her faith with others through her stunning gift of communication. I asked her to endorse a Bible study I had written on the life of Joseph, and she was excited to lend her enthusiastic approval. As she perused the manuscript, she was captivated by the word *hineni* and embraced it as her very own. She sent me a text message asking if I minded if she used *hineni* as her "word of the year" and I giggled while reading her sweet words.

"Cindy," I replied. "It's God's word, not mine! Go for it, sister!" And she did.

Hineni was Cindy's word of the year for 2023 not knowing that she would be diagnosed with cancer in February and be in the presence of the Lord by the end of March. Cindy's *hineni* was a word of surrender and enthusiasm, birthed in a simple desire to obey the Lord.

Do you have a "word of the year"? What is it?

_____

_____

LIFE QUOTE

All I have to offer God this year is… me. Just as I am—imperfect, occasionally outspoken, often weary, but still enthusiastic and deeply willing. Wholehearted. Available.

—Lucinda Secrest McDowell

VERSE OF THE DAY

Samuel was lying down in the temple of the Lord *where the ark of God was, that the* Lord *called Samuel; and he said, "Here I am."*   —1 Samuel 3:3–4

MEANINGFUL MOMENT

Intentionally have a rich conversation with someone you both love and respect. Ask this person what God is doing in their heart and life.

DAILY DECLARATION

"Today and every day I will say, 'Hineni.'"

24

READ

I attended a one-room schoolhouse the first two years of my formal education—and how I loved the safety and familiarity I felt in that outdated, wooden building. My beloved teacher, Mrs. Dombrowski, was an Australian war bride who never had children of her own, so she took all of us—students in kindergarten through grade six—under her loving and warm tutelage.

When I began the second grade, however, I rode a bus to the consolidated school about fifteen minutes from my home. I was a shy, introverted little girl who only wanted to stay at home. The first day I attended the *big school*, as I called it, my mom agreed to drive me to school rather than have me take the bus.

As I walked up the flight of massive stairs to the second floor of the intimidating building, I held tightly to my mother's hand. Tears were quietly falling down my seven-year-old cheeks and I was trembling all over. Although my mom left me in the capable hands of my beloved teacher, I was quaking with fear.

By Friday of the first week of school, Mrs. Dombrowski, who had been my teacher at the one-room school and continued in that role at the consolidated school, knew I was not coping well. She took my small face in her reassuring hands that afternoon and handed me a treasure.

"Carol," she kindly said, "you need a friend. Why don't you take this book home and read it? I think you and Laura will become fast friends."

The book, of course, was *Little House in the Big Woods*, and I was captivated. I read the entire book that weekend; within months, I had devoured Laura Ingalls Wilder's entire series. Then, I was on to *Pippi Longstocking*, *Caddie Woodlawn*, and *All-of-a-Kind Family*.

My adventure into the world of literature had begun and I was forever changed by the power of the written word.

Other than the Bible, what is your favorite book?

_____

_____

Why do you think I included the verb "read" in this book?

_____

_____

What was your favorite book as a child?

_____

_____

TO READ OR NOT TO READ

Some of us truly love the indescribable pleasure that reading offers. I have found great solace, education, challenge, and encouragement on the pages of books. I take a book with me wherever I go so I can read in the doctor's office, at the airport, or in a hotel room.

- If you want to grow as a person, you will read.
- If you want to learn something new, you will read.
- If you want to travel to other lands, you will read.
- If you want to travel through time, you will read.
- If you want to be informed, you will read.
- If you want to be a good conversationalist, you will read.
- If you want to grow in your faith, you will read.

What is your favorite genre of book to read? Mystery? Devotional? Biography?

_____

_____

Do you have a favorite author?

_____

_____

WORDS AND GOD

The Hebrew word *davar*, which is translated as "word," appears in the Bible more than 1,450 times. *Davar* can also be translated as "speak, commandment, promise, and to act."[5]

Words are important in the kingdom of God. It was the Word of God that created the sun, moon, roses, giraffes, and the Grand Teton Mountain Range. The spoken word of God flung the stars into space and separated the continents from the water. With the spoken word, God created everything out of nothing.

The psalmist tells us that creation speaks and declares the glory of God. My heart leaps as I consider the enormous exchange that is happening between God and His creation. God speaks creation into existence and creation speaks of His glory in response. I marvel even as I *davar* those words.

> *The heavens tell of the glory of God; and their expanse declares the work of His hands.*   —Psalm 19:1

When Jesus came to earth as a baby, *"the Word became flesh, and dwelt among us"* (John 1:14).

---

5. Dave Adamson, *52 Hebrew Words Every Christian Should Know* (Bloomingdale, IL: Christian Art Gifts, 2018), 55.

Both the written word and the spoken word are vital components in the kingdom of God. Jesus told stories or parables when He walked among us to teach eternal lessons.

Whether you consider yourself a reader or not, I hope you will reconsider your daily disciplines and spend time every day with your nose in a good book. You might discover that you will lose yourself within its pages ... only to find yourself again.

WALKING WITH THE WISE

There have been times in my life when I have wished I could speak with an expert—an expert gardener, chef, or musician. I hoped to learn from their experiences and gain wisdom from their insight.

There have also been moments when I desired to interrogate people from history, like Abraham Lincoln, Mother Teresa, or Ruth Bell Graham. How I longed to spend an afternoon drinking tea with Corrie ten Boom, Clara Barton, or William Tyndale.

And then, as I pondered their lives and my personal connection with each of them, I realized it was possible to spend time together through the world of literature. Although I will never meet these people in person this side of heaven's shores, I can learn from them as I read the books written about them. The wisdom of these heroes and heroines of the faith will live on through the volumes written about their amazing and faith-filled lives.

One who walks with wise people will be wise.
—Proverbs 13:20

If you could spend time with anyone from history, who would it be?

_____

_____

What questions would you ask this person?

_____

_____

REASONABLE REASONS

If you still aren't convinced that the commitment to read will add a dynamic component to your life, allow me to share some research with you that just might change your mind.

+ Reading is good for your brain. Scientific studies show that reading makes you smarter, increases your blood flow, and improves connectivity in the brain.

+ Reading introduces you to new ideas and helps with problem-solving skills.

+ Reading improves conversational skills as well as vocabulary.

+ Reading strengthens your worldview and convictions.

+ Reading improves your attention span.

+ Reading improves your knowledge of history.

+ Reading increases cultural knowledge without an expensive plane flight.

+ Reading challenges your imagination.

+ Reading increases your skill in an area of interest.

+ Reading inspires you.

+ Reading reduces stress.[6]

6. Ariel Abke, "12 Reasons You Should Read (At Least) 12 Books This Year," Pearson, August 30, 2020, www.pearsonaccelerated.com/blog/12-reasons-you-should-read-at-least-12-books-this-year.

IT'S A JOURNEY

If you struggle with a desire to read, perhaps these few suggestions will get you started on your journey:

+ Choose a time to read that fits into your schedule. I always take fifteen to twenty minutes at lunchtime and read just for enjoyment. I also love to read in bed at night before I turn out the light.

+ I ask my friends what they are reading and what they would suggest I might enjoy reading.

+ I make a list of books on Amazon, on Audible, and on Kindle that I hope to read over the coming year.

+ I have reading partners who read the same book I am reading so we can share our thoughts and discuss it.

UP TO YOU!

I don't know what habits or interests have enhanced your life, but reading has changed me in a way that little else has. While I am walking in the morning, I am listening to a book; before I sleep at night, I read a riveting book; when I take my lunch break, I open the pages of a book.

I can travel through time and across continents without leaving the warmth and safety of my own home. I am the woman I am today because I have chosen to be a woman who reads.

What interests other than reading have filled the days of your life?

_____

_____

LIFE QUOTE

In reading great literature I become a thousand men and yet remain myself. ... I transcend myself; and am never more myself than when I do.   —C. S. Lewis

VERSE OF THE DAY

In the beginning was the Word, and the Word was with God, and the Word was God.   —John 1:1

MEANINGFUL MOMENT

If you could write a book, what would the title be? What would the book be about?

DAILY DECLARATION

"I declare that I will make the time to read often during my week. I will choose my books wisely and listen for God's voice as I read."

25

WAIT

What do you do when you find yourself *in the wait?* We have all been there, haven't we? Waiting is a test, often presented by the loving Father, intended to help His dear children lean more fully upon His power and His promises. I must admit, however, I am among the Lord's most impatient children. And so, daily I wait.

+ Waiting for God to answer.
+ Waiting for mountains to move.
+ Waiting for provision.
+ Waiting for healing.
+ Waiting for breakthrough.
+ Waiting for the storm to pass.
+ Waiting for dreams to come true.
+ Waiting for someone ... anyone ... to notice that I am *in the wait.*

No one likes to wait. However, we are all continuously waiting for something to happen or for someone to change. Waiting never ends ... but goes on and on and on through all the seasons of life.

Ordinary days drag by as we set our hearts and minds on the impossible possibilities of tomorrow. The conundrum is that I suspect I don't have time to wait—and yet the wait drags on. After all, time waits for no one so why should I?

We wait.

Tap our toes.

Check our watches or our phones.

Look at the calendar.

Roll our eyes.

Sigh.

Try to pray.

Eat a piece of chocolate.

Scroll through social media.

As I am waiting, it is my personal choice whether I will wait well or wait poorly. Much of life is about what we do with the time spent in the wait.

What are you currently waiting for?

_____

_____

Do you believe that prayer can change the length of the wait?

_____

_____

DON'T DO IT!

I am probably just a bit like Thomas Edison, who declared that he had not failed after a series of experiments were unsuccessful. Instead, he said, "I have gotten a lot of results! I know several thousand things that won't work."

Taking a tip from Edison, I can say, "I am not impatient. I have just discovered 10,000 ways how *not* to wait."

First, I have learned you should not worry while you wait. Worrying is a waste of valuable time, vital energy, and emotional health. Worry carries with it no intrinsic problem-solving ability but negates thoughts that could be given to hopeful expectation. Worry will warp your today and threaten your tomorrow. Worry changes nothing, and it destroys your peace and joy.

I have had to remind myself often that the definition of prayer is not *worrying on my knees.* I have heard it said that worrying is thinking the thoughts of the enemy while trust is thinking the thoughts of God. Oh! How I long to think like God thinks—especially when I am waiting.

Second, don't be negative while you wait. Don't conjure up every worst-case scenario and dwell upon the devastation that might be around the corner of your life. While you are waiting, throw away negativity like yesterday's garbage. Negativity stirs up a vile and putrid odor that ruins the glory of today. Don't allow the impatience you are feeling to come explosively tumbling out of your mouth.

Third, don't gossip and criticize others while you wait. If you compare your life to someone else's life while you are in the wait, you will lose the sight of your own blessings.

I've often been found guilty of wasting my life while spending time in the wait. I fritter away hours wishing my life was somehow different rather than using those same hours in meaningful pursuits.

And finally, don't become bitter while you wait. Bitterness often turns into anger, which is a devastating way to try to make it through the wait.

How have you waited poorly over the years?

_____

_____

What are some emotions you have experienced while waiting?

_____

_____

JUST DO IT!

Now that you know how *not* to wait, I can assure you that the possibilities of waiting well are endless.

- Invest yourself in productive and healthy activities such as walking or biking.
- Volunteer at a homeless shelter.
- Babysit for a young family.
- Take an elderly couple out to lunch and ask them what they have learned about marriage.
- Go on mission trips.
- Invite people into your home for dinner and a game night.
- Pray for others while you wait.
- Write notes of encouragement to others who are waiting.

One of the most valuable disciplines I have cultivated while in the waiting room of life is to talk the language of hope. Every time I am tempted to whine or complain, I stop myself immediately and change my language to that of hope. Hope should be the native tongue of someone who is waiting. Learn to speak *hope* just like you would learn to speak a new language before visiting a foreign country. The only language that should be spoken in the waiting room of life is the language of hope.

And finally, worship your way through the wait. Choose to sing yourself to sleep at night and whistle while you work. Hum while you pray and keep a symphony of genuine joy stirring while you are waiting for God to complete His work on your behalf. The song of your heart should be at its loudest when you find yourself in the waiting room of life. A seemingly endless wait should never silence the song of your life but should turn it up to resounding and echoing proportions. The most powerful song is always heard right before the dawn of a new day!

Wait for the LORD*; be strong and let your heart take courage;*
yes, wait for the LORD. —Psalm 27:14

What are some healthy habits you have developed while waiting?

_____

_____

Is there a Scripture verse or lyrics to a song that have helped you to wait well?

_____

_____

WHY WAIT?

In his preface to *Mere Christianity*, C. S. Lewis compares waiting to being in a hall with many closed doors while trying to find a church or denomination that fits:

> It is true that some people may find they have to wait in the hall for a considerable time, while others feel certain almost at once which door they must knock at. I do not know why there is this difference, but I am sure God keeps no one waiting unless He sees that it is good for him to wait. When you do get into your room you will find that the long wait has done you some kind of good which you would not have had otherwise. But you must regard it as waiting, not as camping. You must keep on praying for light: and, of course, even in the hall, you must begin trying to obey the rules which are common to the whole house. And above all you must be asking which door is the true one; not which pleases you best by its paint and panelling.

As I ponder all the endless hours I have spent in the waiting room of life, I can assure you that God keeps no one waiting unless He desires to do a strengthening work in their lives. When your time in the waiting room is finally complete, you will find you have matured and that a rich wisdom has become part of your character that was not there before.

I wonder if we must not view *waiting* for waiting's sake alone, but as a time set aside for growth and instruction. Perhaps the waiting room just may be the most exacting classroom in which we will ever spend time. While you wait, your life is not on pause but is being groomed and tutored for what is yet to come by the hand of God.

I wonder if the wait is more a place of power and less a place of weakness than I first perceived it to be. The days—even the years—that I have spent waiting are the very times I have found myself on my knees or on my face in His dear presence. I always find joy in His presence, even in the wait. The slowly passing hours that I have spent waiting have offered me the gift of spending more time in His refreshing Word. The sacred pages of Scripture speak to me and give me new direction while I am in the wait. The months I have spent waiting for the hand of God to move have increased the volume of the song of my heart. Worship never ceases to remove my focus from what I am lacking to be firmly set on who He is in glory and splendor.

While I am waiting, I discover that I am not alone but that He is with me in the wait. There is no one I would rather wait with than Him! He never becomes frustrated with me or with my frustration. I find it a far more powerful choice to simply wait with Him than to wait for His hand to move. It's in the wait that my life is joined to eternity's focus, to heaven's power, and to His perpetual love.

What are some of the benefits you have experienced from spending time waiting?

_____

_____

LIFE QUOTE

Biblically, waiting is not just something we have to do until we get what we want. Waiting is part of the process of becoming what God wants us to be.   —John Ortberg

VERSE OF THE DAY

Do you not know? Have you not heard? The Everlasting God, the LORD, *the Creator of the ends of the earth does not become weary or tired. His understanding is unsearchable. He gives strength to the weary, and to the one who lacks might He increases power. Though youths grow weary and tired, and vigorous young men stumble badly, yet those who wait for the* LORD *will gain new strength; they will mount up with wings like eagles, they will run and not get tired, they will walk and not become weary.*

—Isaiah 40:28–31

MEANINGFUL MOMENT

Pray for someone else today who is waiting. Encourage this person in a practical and hopeful way.

DAILY DECLARATION

"I declare today that I will wait well. I will stay in the Word, I will pray, I will sing, and I will trust."

26

OVERCOME

There have been times in life when I have seen trouble, conflict, or disappointment headed my way. In those awful moments, I have screamed, curled into the fetal position, or gone shopping. I have also panicked, believing my boat was about to sink and what was about to happen would surely be the very worst days of my entire life. My friend, I could have written those infamous books, *Worst Case Scenarios, Carol and the Horrible, No Good, Very Bad Day,* or *War and Peace.*

I have falsely believed the battle ahead would maim me or subtract from my life; I have assumed that I would be wounded or paralyzed by the warfare I was about to engage in. I just knew that the combat zone I was entering would ensure that I would never reach my destiny in Christ.

When I have faced battles in the past, there have been times I have felt insignificant, forgotten by God, and trapped by the enemy. However, several years ago when I was battling cancer, God captured my attention and revolutionized my warped thinking patterns. This is what I heard the Father say as I was fighting for my very life:

+ What if a battle was meant to be your finest hour?

+ What if it was in a battle that you discovered your true significance?

+ What if you received treasures from a battle that you never would have received otherwise?

I now believe the contests we are called to fight this side of heaven and overcome are meant to promote not paralyze us. Battles were meant to add to our significance rather than subtract from our identity.

The call to fight well and to face a battle with courage and resolve is a vital aspect of the abundant life you have been invited to live.

- Why would you want an easy life when you could live where fiery darts are flying and where you are winning as you declare the dynamic Word of God?

- Why would you want to tiptoe through the tulips when you could be charging the enemy with the power of the Holy Spirit?

- Why would you want to settle for mundane when God wants you to be more than a conqueror?

Battles can exponentially, miraculously, and undeniably add to your significance as a child of God. We serve a God who is able to use every battle, every moment of warfare, and every fiery dart of the enemy for a greater good than we could ever imagine.

> But in all these things we are more than conquerors, through him
> that loved us.   —Romans 8:37 WEB

You will never be an overcomer if you don't go to battle. You will never be identified as *more than a conqueror* if you haven't had the opportunity to conquer something. You won't be led in triumphant procession if you have never had the opportunity to be triumphant.

What do you believe has been your finest hour in life?

_____

_____

Make a list of a few of the things you have overcome in life:

1. _____

2. _____

3. _____

4. _____

WHY FIGHT?

Jeremiah was a faithful and obedient servant of the Lord who was called as a young man to be a prophet. While the Lord was explaining this call to him, the Lord also prepared him for the troubling days ahead:

> "They will fight against you but they will not overcome you, for I am with you to save you," declares the LORD. —Jeremiah 1:19

There is no one alive today who can accomplish what you and God are able to accomplish together. No matter what battle you are in today, He is with you. God has assigned battles to you just as He assigned them to Jeremiah. When you are in the heat of the battle, always remember that the Lord is with you to deliver you, just as He was with Jeremiah.

Why would the Lord allow one of His dearly loved daughters or specifically chosen sons to fight in an outrageous and difficult battle? The simple answer to that question is because we live in a fallen world that is filled with pain and evil. God needs someone—someone just like you and just like me—to apply the victory of Jesus Christ to the broken places in this desperate world.

- One of my battle assignments is to pray for women dealing with infertility.
- One of my battle assignments is to pray for people fighting depression.
- One of my battle assignments is to pray for women who are battling cancer.
- One of my battle assignments is to stand in faith with moms of prodigal children.
- One of my battle assignments is to pray for millennials to come back to their faith.

When we realize that a battle is meant to be our finest hour, it revolutionizes every challenge and every heartache into places where we apply the power of God for a resounding victory. You will have battles and opposition this side of heaven's glory, but the Lord will be with you in every hard place and in every fierce competition.

When you live in your calling, you will face an angry enemy—always. God is not surprised when one of His children faces opposition. However, remember that your enemy will not overcome you because the Lord is with you to deliver you.

The words the Lord spoke to Jeremiah thousands of years ago are yours to embrace today. "*I am with you to save you*" may be among the most significant words in Scripture, and they are yours.

Make a list of some of your battle assignments as I did with mine.

1. _____

2. _____

3. _____

4. _____

5. _____

What is one habit you ascribe to daily as part of your overcoming strategy?

_____

_____

THE JOY OF THE BATTLE

Teddy Roosevelt was a larger-than-life president whose image is chiseled into Mount Rushmore in the South Dakota mountains.

Before he was president of the United States of America, Teddy led the Rough Riders up the San Juan Hill during the Spanish-American War. Reporters detail the fact that machine gun bullets sprayed out of the top of the mountain, cutting down soldier after soldier, yet Teddy fought on always urging his men forward. It was in that terrible moment of a vicious and barbaric battle that he discovered what he called the "power of joy in battle."

A witness that day said in that awful moment, Teddy became the most magnificent soldier he had ever seen. A shell exploded near him, burning his skin, but Teddy fought on. A stray bullet nicked his elbow, but Teddy didn't even notice. He refused to stop fighting until the battle was won. For the rest of his life, Roosevelt said July 1, 1898, was the greatest day of his life because he had discovered that joy.

Do you believe it is possible to have "joy in a battle"? Why or why not?

_____

_____

Have you ever experienced joy in a battle?

_____

_____

WHERE IS THE JOY?

If you want to discover the power of joy in a battle, as President Roosevelt and I both have, you will fight with the weapons given to you by the One who knows you best and loves you most. You will not fight with your emotions, but you will fight by obeying the principles of Scripture. How wonderful to know that the One who wrote our fighting manual has never lost a battle yet!

PRAYER

With every prayer and request, pray at all times in the Spirit, and with this in view, be alert with all perseverance and every request for all the saints.   —Ephesians 6:18

Daniel prayed. The lions' den was no match for a man of prayer. It was his finest hour. (See Daniel 6:21–22.)

Paul and Silas prayed in prison until their chains broke and the walls shook with an earthquake. It was their finest hour. (See Acts 16:25–26.)

Jonah prayed in the belly of a great fish, and the fish burped him up on dry ground. It was Jonah's finest hour. (See Jonah 2.)

Your battle will either be a place of defeat or a place of prayer. You decide.

THE WORD OF GOD

And take the helmet of salvation and the sword of the Spirit, which is the word of God.   —Ephesians 6:17

When I am in a battle, I find a fighting verse and I declare it out loud daily. I share it with anyone who will listen and even with those who don't want to listen. I sing my fighting verse; I write this verse on various pieces of paper and post it all over my house. Every time I say my fighting verse out loud, the enemy must hear it, and it is a fatal lash with the sword of the Spirit.

Jesus declared the Word of God to the enemy in the wilderness, and it became a place of grand significance. If Jesus can't win a battle without declaring the Word of God out loud then neither can we.

A battle becomes your finest hour when you declare the Word of God.

WORSHIP

I will bless the LORD at all times; His praise shall continually be in my mouth.   —Psalm 34:1

We give a victory shout before the victory has been won in the natural.

We sing in the rain and in the furnace of great affliction.

Our song will always be louder than the lies of the enemy.

There is no battle that will mute the song of the redeemed of the Lord.

LIFE QUOTE

The greater the difficulty to be overcome, the more it will be seen how much can be accomplished by prayer and faith.

—George Müller

VERSE OF THE DAY

*For whoever has been born of God overcomes the world; and this is the victory that has **overcome** the world: our faith.*

—1 John 5:4

MEANINGFUL MOMENT

Do you know anyone who is in a battle today? Reach out to this person right now and pray for them. Give this friend a Scripture verse to hang onto during the battle.

DAILY DECLARATION

"I declare that I am more than a conqueror in Christ Jesus and that He will never leave me no matter what battle I might be facing."

27

TRUST

It was the darkest hour of my young life. Although Craig and I had two precious boys whom I loved more than life itself, I still ached to enlarge our family. I was able to get pregnant, but my body was unable to stay pregnant. My pregnancies all began with a healthy baby. However, between twelve and twenty weeks in five successive pregnancies, each baby died inside my womb. I held four of those little lives in my hand. My heart was broken, my hormones were raging, and my arms were empty.

As Christmas approached that awful year, I didn't have the energy to direct the annual church choral program as was normally my joyful habit. A dear friend offered to do it for me, and I accepted her suggestion gratefully. She even recommended that she could choose all the music as well as find an accompanist. I was off the holiday hook knowing my heart was struggling to celebrate what most people refer to as "the most wonderful time of the year."

On Christmas Sunday, I walked into the church pastored by my husband, with a little boy on each side of me. I was trying not to cry because I had expected to be holding a newborn baby in my arms that final Sunday of Advent. As the choir stood poised and ready to perform, my friend announced to the small but wonderful church family, "We are dedicating our performance today to Carol, who has taught us all how to trust the Lord."

Of course, then, the tears ran down my cheeks unabated while two growing boys looked anxiously up at their brokenhearted mama. I don't remember much about the notes the choir sang that day or even what specific songs were part of their repertoire. However, I do recall the lyrics to the final song of the Christmas cantata:

"God is too wise to be mistaken.

God is too good to be unkind.

So when you don't understand

When You don't see His plan

When you can't see His hand,

Trust His heart."

In that moment, I knew I could trust His heart although I was unable to see His plan. I was able to rejoice knowing He was good and wise. My broken heart began to heal that day and even I could lift my voice and sing, "Joy to the world, the Lord has come!"

What is your definition of the word "trust"?

_____

_____

What has been the most difficult moment in your life to trust the Lord?

_____

_____

THE CHARACTER OF GOD

Trust is our response to the character of God. When you know who He is and what His promises are, trust will be as instinctive as breathing in and breathing out. When you focus on His goodness and remember His faithfulness, trust will spring out of your soul exuberantly and lavishly.

However, if you doubt Him or wonder if He is merciful and kind, trust will always be a struggle for you. As believers in Christ, we must take the time to know Him in His fullness and power. We know Him as we spend time in His Word and as we listen for His dear voice. I hope you understand that part of the delight of living an abundant life is found in simply getting to know the Lord, your Father and your Creator.

You must know Him to trust Him; you must be amazed at who He is before you can put your full confidence in Him. Once you take the time to know Him—to intimately know Him in His splendor and in His wonder—trust will be a glorious reflexive response to His nature.

> *And those who know Your name will put their **trust** in You, for You, LORD, have not abandoned those who seek You.*
>
> —Psalm 9:10

How can you get to know the Lord more intimately?

_____

_____

Write down three to five components of the Lord's character below:

1. _____

2. _____

3. _____

4. _____

5. _____

THE BENEFIT OF TRUST

So many people pray for inner peace amidst outward turmoil; they beg God to remove their unease and anxiety. However, I believe there is a more powerful antidote that will overcome worry than prayer is able to provide. The miraculous antidote of which I speak is sincere trust. You will never have peace in your heart apart from an intentional trust in the Lord.

The steadfast of mind You will keep in perfect peace, because he trusts in You. —Isaiah 26:3

Trust is not a feeling, but it is a spiritual discipline. I can trust the Lord when I don't like my circumstances and when I don't understand what I am going through. My goal in traveling through a desert experience in life is not to understand why I am there but to obtain the peace that passes all understanding. (See Philippians 4:7.) The way I am able to acquire this supernatural, miraculous, God-birthed peace is when I trust Him without reserve.

LET'S START AT THE BEGINNING

It has been my experience that trust often begins in my mouth. Even when I don't feel it, I can say, "Lord, I trust You. I know You are good. I know You care about me and so I will trust You."

As I confess my trust in Him, an inward miracle begins to happen in my soul. As my mouth reminds my heart of who God is, the trust comes rolling in. I remind myself what God has done in the past and who the Word of God says He is. As I speak and think about the character of God and what He has promised me, trust becomes more than an emotion; it becomes an inner resolve.

When I am assailed by doubts and peace is nowhere to be found, I can lean into the immutable truth of His Word.

The LORD will accomplish what concerns me; Your faithfulness, LORD, is everlasting; do not abandon the works of Your hands. —Psalm 138:8

What does the promise, "The Lord will accomplish what concerns me" mean to you?

_____

_____

What does it mean to you personally that the Lord's faithfulness is "everlasting"?

_____

_____

HOW WONDERFUL TO KNOW!

When I am struggling with worry or anxiety and can't seem to corral my thoughts or control my tongue, I like to participate in an activity I have aptly named, "How wonderful to know!" This spiritual discipline of mine is one of the most direct avenues to trust you will ever walk upon. In this trust-building activity, I write out all the remarkable attributes of the character of God and all of the marvelous promises in the Bible that I can think of prefaced by the words, "How wonderful to know…"

+ How wonderful to know He has promised never to leave me or forsake me!

+ How wonderful to know that no one will ever love me like Jesus!

+ How wonderful to know that His mercies are new every morning!

+ How wonderful to know that His faithfulness extends to a thousand generations!

+ How wonderful to know that He wins every battle He fights.

+ How wonderful to know that greater is He who is in me than he who is in the world.

As I recite and remember who He is and what the Word of God has declared, my trust levels rise, and I am filled with a tangible faith. Worries fly away and anxiety disappears because I have set my mind on Him and all that He is.

Now it's your turn. Write out five "How wonderful to know ..."
statements of your own.

1. _____

2. _____

3. _____

4. _____

5. _____

LIFE QUOTE

When you cannot see an inch before you, trust in Him that is, that was, and is to come. ... If you trust in an unchanging God, whose love, and faithfulness, and power cannot be diminished, however dark your way may be, then you have a glorious object for your faith to rest upon!

—Charles Spurgeon

VERSE OF THE DAY

Trust in the LORD and do good; live in the land and cultivate faithfulness. Delight yourself in the LORD; and He will give you the desires of your heart. Commit your way to the LORD, trust also in Him, and He will do it.   —Psalm 37:3–5

MEANINGFUL MOMENT

Write out a prayer of complete trust in the Lord. This is a purposeful way to erase your anxiety and fear.

DAILY DECLARATION

"I declare that today is a great day to trust the Lord! I know who my God is, I believe His promises, and I will trust Him with my life today."

28

OBEY

When Craig and I were deciding what hymns would be sung at our wedding, the list was short but meaningful. We quickly narrowed it down to two anthems that had been sung by thousands of saints and sinners for a century or more before our marriage ceremony. We invited our families, friends, and loved ones to join us in singing, "Great Is Thy Faithfulness" as a stirring declaration to who God is. Then, later in the service, everyone stood to their feet and prayerfully sang, "Trust and Obey" as we made our commitment to Him.

> When we walk with the Lord
> in the light of His word,
> what a glory He sheds on our way!
> While we do His good will,
> He abides with us still,
> and with all who will trust and obey.
> Trust and obey, for there's no other way
> to be happy in Jesus, but to trust and obey.[7]

I wonder if our entire Christian walk of faith can be boiled down to those two short yet convicting words: *trust* and *obey*.

What is your favorite hymn of faith?

_____

_____

---

7. John H. Sammis, "Trust and Obey," 1887.

If you are married or have been married, what is your favorite memory of your wedding day?

_____

_____

If you have never been married, spend some time praying for your friends' marriages.

CHILDREN

When my children were young, we taught them the value of obeying right away, all the way, and in a happy way. If immediate, thorough, and heartfelt obedience is vital for children in a family, so it is for all of us in the family of God.

If I asked a child to help me with the dishes, and they ignored my request, I asked patiently again. Often the answer was something like, "I'll be right there, Mama. I need to finish this TV show." At that time, it was important for me to remind this precious but distracted child, "Delayed obedience is disobedience."

One day, as I was dealing with frustrating behavior by one of my young children, the Lord used that moment as a teaching moment in my life. He reminded me of something He had asked me to do months earlier that I had not yet followed through on. My intentions were good; I loved to obey the Lord. However, I had just not found the time to do what the Lord had required of me. I heard the Holy Spirit whisper into the depths of my heart, "Carol, what is true for your children is true for you as well. Delayed obedience is disobedience."

You are a child of God, and He will ask you to do things that are inconvenient, difficult, demanding, and time-consuming. We must obey immediately, thoroughly, and wholeheartedly. Love requires no less.

Not a burden we bear,
not a sorrow we share,

but our toil He doth richly repay;
not a grief or a loss,
not a frown or a cross,
but is blest if we trust and obey.[8]

In what area of your life do you have a difficult time obeying the Lord?

_____

_____

Why is thorough obedience so important to our Christian walk?

_____

_____

I LOVE HIM

As a child, I desired to obey my parents because I loved them so dearly. I never wanted to participate in activities or conversations that would bring pain to their hearts. Even as a teenager, while others were experimenting with sex, drugs, and alcohol, I would look into my father's warm, brown eyes and know I could never do anything to disappoint him. He loved me unconditionally and although I knew his love was more dynamic than my failures, I still yearned to please him.

Just as trust is the litmus test for how well we know the Lord, perhaps obedience is the test for how deep our love is for Him.

Focusing on your love for the Lord will enable you to embrace obedience as a delightful and fulfilling part of your life. If you give Him your whole heart, your time, and your thought life, you will develop a joyful bent toward obedience.

_____

8. Ibid.

Obeying the Father was never meant to be a legalistic approach to life or a list of right and wrong. True obedience from the heart is at once fulfilling and restorative; obedience birthed from love sustains us in storm-tossed waters and lights the way in the darkest night.

YES!

One of the spiritual disciplines that I have fully embraced over the past decade is choosing a *Word of the Year* annually. It's been a wonderful way for me to begin a new year as I prayerfully consider what areas of my life need strengthening as well as what God might have planned for me in the coming year. I also thoroughly enjoy the opportunity to hear God's voice in fresh and new ways.

A few years ago, as I was praying about my word for the newly birthed 365 days, I heard the Lord say, "Yes." As I examined my heart and prayer life, I wondered which one of my many prayers He was responding to in the affirmative.

I continued to pray about my assigned word, writing down all sorts of ideas with Scripture references beside each possible word. As the hours passed by, I continued to hear the Lord say, "Yes."

I thought to myself, "Thank You, Lord. Thank You that You are affirming, 'Yes, Carol, I have a word for you in the coming year.'" And then, I had a moment of clarity. The Lord had been repeatedly telling me that my Word for the Year was "Yes!" What a marvelous word it was!

+ Every time the Lord asked me to serve someone, I could instantly say, "Yes!"

+ Every time the Lord asked me to surrender something, I could gladly say, "Yes!"

+ Every time the Lord gave me a new assignment, my enthusiastic response was, "Yes!"

During my *Yes Year*, as I have come to call it, I learned the satisfaction and the thrill of immediate and unquestioning obedience to His will, His Word, and His ways.

Then in fellowship sweet
we will sit at His feet,
or we'll walk by His side in the way;
what He says we will do,
where He sends we will go;
never fear, only trust and obey.
Trust and obey, for there's no other way
to be happy in Jesus, but to trust and obey.[9]

LIFE QUOTE

I believe Christians often perceive obedience to God as some test designed just to see if we're really committed to Him. But what if it's designed as God's way of giving us what's best for us?   —Craig Groeschel

VERSE OF THE DAY

I delight to do Your will, my God; Your Law is within my heart.   —Psalm 40:8

MEANINGFUL MOMENT

Spend some time listening for the Lord's voice today. Ask Him how you can obey Him. Respond with an immediate and enthusiastic, "Yes!"

DAILY DECLARATION

"I love You, Lord. And because I love You with my whole heart, I will obey Your Word."

---

9. Ibid.

29

BE

My friend, it is time for the action of your life to settle into your very identity. Perhaps the grandest discovery of a life well-lived is when the *doing* becomes the *being* of an individual.

Every verb we have addressed thus far has been an action verb, a verb that shows continued or progressive action by the subject of the sentence.

Now, however, it is time to consider the verb *be*. In traditional grammar, a verb of being does not show action but instead identifies who or what the subject is, was, or will be. I pray that your *doing* will now infiltrate your very *being*.

+ You no longer merely worship from time to time; instead, you have become a passionate worshipper.

+ No longer is encouraging others an assignment on your daily to-do list, but you are identified as an enthusiastic encourager.

+ Offering forgiveness to others is no longer what you do, but forgiveness is the consuming identification of every cell in your body.

+ Determining whether to obey the Lord no longer causes a civil war in your soul, but you are the Lord's obedient child.

+ Giving is not an action, but generosity is written upon your heart.

You are a beloved child of God, and your identity has been determined by the One who knows you best and loves you most. Performing appropriately is not the demonstration of your identity but having His blood coursing through your veins and allowing your heart to beat in sweet synchronization with His heart changes who you are. You are His, and He determines your thought life, your emotional responses, and your actions. You have become like Him as you surrender all you are to Him.

IT'S A PROCESS

The *being* aspect of your identity in Christ happened the moment you were born again and chose to follow Him completely. In that glorious, miraculous moment of undeserved forgiveness, you were made new and redeemed.

> *Therefore if anyone is in Christ, this person is a new creation; the old things passed away; behold, new things have come.*
> —2 Corinthians 5:17

+ You are no longer a sinner, but you are now known as a saint.

+ You are no longer a prodigal, but you are the beloved child.

+ You are the righteousness of God in Jesus Christ.

+ You are a blessing.

+ You are the apple of His eye.

+ You are the light of the world.

However, becoming like Him is a process—and what a glorious process it is!

CONSTANTLY BECOMING

> *Therefore be imitators of God, as beloved children.*
> —Ephesians 5:1

The word "imitators" in this memorable verse is the translation of the Greek word *mimetes*. As you may have guessed, the word *mimetes* means "to imitate someone or to mimic what you see someone else doing." *Mimetes* can also describe emulating a teacher, parent, or another role model. In ancient days, when a person was respected for his or her noble character, others were encouraged to emulate this worthy person.[10]

Paul is encouraging us, in these verses penned two thousand years ago, to model our lives after God and to become like Him. We are called to wholeheartedly become like the One who made us and who loves us.

Paul begins this verse with the Greek word *ginomai* or "therefore," which helps this phrase to mean, "Be constantly in the process of becoming more like God."[11]

God wants His children to become more like Christ daily. It is the will of God for the people of God. Becoming like Christ is not accomplished simply in the *doing*; becoming like Christ is when the *doing* is overshadowed by the *being*.

> *But whoever keeps His word, in him the love of God has truly been perfected. By this we know that we are in Him: the one who says that he remains in Him ought, himself also, walk just as He walked.*   —1 John 2:5–6

AUTHENTIC CHRISTLIKENESS

When Jesus lived on planet Earth in the flesh, He caused a revolution with only twelve disciples. They changed the way women were viewed, they confronted the religious power brokers, they wrestled with the governmental authority figures, they brought honor to lepers, and they went about doing good. What changes could we make today if we truly lived the way Jesus lived?

There is a story told of a professor in India who realized during a class discussion that one of his students identified as a Christian. The professor, who was known as part of the academic elite in the Hindu world, looked the young man in the eyes and challenged him,

---

10. Renner, *Sparkling Gems from the Greek*, 137.
11. Ibid., 138.

"If you Christians lived like Jesus Christ, India would be at your feet tomorrow."

There is yet another story from the Islamic world attributed to the Reverend Iskandar Jadeed, a former Arab Muslim. He has been famously quoted as saying, "If all Christians were Christians—that is Christlike—there would be no more Islam today."

My friend, you might change the world when you decide to be like Christ.

I CAN'T

Is it possible for a human being like you or me to become Christlike in every action, every word, and every thought? In our own strength, it is impossible. There is no human way to attain this extraordinary challenge of becoming like our Lord.

How wonderful to know that when Jesus went to heaven, He gave us the Holy Spirit to dwell within us and to complete the work of transformation. The Holy Spirit will change us from within.

> *I will ask the Father, and He will give you another Helper, so that He may be with you forever; the Helper is the Spirit of truth, whom the world cannot receive, because it does not see Him or know Him; but you know Him because He remains with you and will be in you.* —John 14:16–17

We can be like Him when the power of the Holy Spirit dwells within us. It is not a transformation enacted by verbs or behavior, but it is the quiet melding of my will to His. The Holy Spirit will give me the mind of Christ so I will think His thoughts. When the Holy Spirit empowers me, it is then that I decrease so that Christ, in me, will increase to full authority and chosen identity.

A PARABLE OF BEING

A king loved to visit his garden in the early morning hours of each new day. One day, as he opened his garden gate, he found all his lovely trees and flowers were drooping and fading away.

This wise king asked the oak, who stood as a sentinel near the entrance, why his leaves were withering, and his branches were dying. "It is because I am not tall and stately like the pine," was the plaintive reply.

The pine tree was bending low while dropping its green needles upon the garden pathway. The king's concern extended to the formerly massive evergreen and asked the pine why it was so melancholy. "It is because I do not bear grapes like the fruitful vines," replied the pine as it mournfully dropped more of its needles on the ground.

The grape vine decided to die because it could not stand tall and straight like the peach tree. The geranium was disconsolate because it wasn't fragrant like the lilac.

Toward the back of the garden was a small slip of heartsease, a flower low to the ground and nearly obscured by all the large trees and blooming bushes. The heartsease had lifted its tiny face to the sun and seemed to bring cheerfulness to its hidden corner.

"Well, well, well," said the kind but powerful king, "I am so thankful that in the middle of this discouraged garden, you seem to be one brave little flower. Why are you not disheartened?"

The heartsease smiled up at the one who had planted him in this particular spot and whispered, "I know I am not as grand as others, but I thought if you had wanted an oak, pine, peach tree, or lilac, you would have planted them here. But you planted me here so I will be the best little heartsease I can be. I will be a heartsease for you, my king."[12]

BE RATHER THAN DO

When you become like Him, every day will be a day of rare delight and unmatched joy. When you choose to know Him, each

---

12. Paraphrased from Cowman, *Streams in the Desert*.

season of life will be a vibrant demonstration of abundant hope and peace. When you allow the Holy Spirit to fill every corner of your small heart, the world will stand to its feet in applause.

You have been created to honor Him and to become like Him. Do it with all your heart.

LIFE QUOTE

Christians need to look like what they are talking about. ... What communicates now is basically personal authenticity.

—John Poulton

VERSE OF THE DAY

But you did not learn Christ in this way, if indeed you have heard Him and have been taught in Him, just as truth is in Jesus, that, in reference to your former way of life, you are to rid yourselves of the old self, which is being corrupted in accordance with the lusts of deceit, and that you are to be renewed in the spirit of your minds, and to put on the new self, which in the likeness of God has been created in righteousness and holiness of the truth.   —Ephesians 4:20–24

MEANINGFUL MOMENT

Spend some time today just drinking in His presence and listening for His voice. Don't *do* anything at all ... just *be*. Lose yourself in His unspeakable love for you.

DAILY DECLARATION

"I declare that today and every day, I will become like Christ. It is my heart's desire."

30

LOVE

How can you begin to build a vibrant and meaningful life without the commitment to love ardently in thought, word, and deed? Love is at the core of Christian faith and must not be watered down by assuming it is an emotional response to another person's beauty or winsome personality.

Love is a command, it is an act of unselfish behavior, and it defines the One who sits on the throne of our hearts. One of the greatest mistakes we make is assuming that love is about me and my preferences; loving the way Christ loved is a lifestyle of sacrificial love and unselfish behavior.

Love is not chocolate candy hearts, rainbows, or flirtatious glances; love is not roses given to celebrate an anniversary nor is it a once-in-a-lifetime declaration. Love is the very essence of eternity meant to revolutionize the history of mankind. Love's power is able to replace animosity or indifference with the compassionate character of God.

Love is the call to be like Christ. It is the command to die to self. Love is the freedom to be who we were created to be.

What is your definition of the word "love"?

Other than the Lord, who has loved you most completely?

DIFFICULT PEOPLE

One of the most glorious assignments you will ever be given is to love a difficult person. Do you know someone who is fractious and frustrating? Are you acquainted with a person who is prideful, selfish, and irritable? We all know these churlish folks and immediately hide when their presence threatens to mar our happy existence.

What if this challenging person is an assignment from God? What if this irascible human being is a gift designed to help you learn how to love with God's kind of love?

The problem is, we have allowed difficult people to bring out the worst in us when they have been placed in our lives to bring out the Jesus in us. You are never more like Jesus than when you are loving an obstinate person. Open wide the windows of your heart and determine to love like Jesus!

I often remind myself that I am the difficult person that Jesus has chosen to love fully.

Do you have a difficult person in your life?

_____

_____

How can you love this person more effectively?

_____

_____

NOT ABOUT ME

Christian love is not for the fulfillment or ease of self, but it is always an opportunity to bring glory to God in our daily and personal choices. When I am called to love someone who is difficult for me to love, it is a miraculous moment when I can decrease and allow the Lord to increase in me and through me.

He must increase, but I must decrease. —John 3:30

If I am unable to apply those words to exacting relationships, then I am unable to apply them anywhere. The love I am called to exhibit as a daughter of God is selfless and generous. God's love is a sacrificial love that refuses to scream while it suffers on behalf of others.

If I mistakenly believe that love exists to meet my needs first, at the exclusion of everyone else, I am allowing the world to warp the most precious gift God has ever given. God generously offered love to a people who didn't deserve His all-consuming, non-negotiable, and eternal compassion. And yet He still gave all that He had to give. I can do no less.

A FINAL WORD

It was the night before Jesus would be betrayed and arrested. He was having one final meal with His band of brothers before His death and resurrection. During this concluding meal, I can imagine He looked around the table at those He had been with for three years. They had laughed together, argued with one another, experienced extraordinary miracles, heard the parables, fought the raging seas, and walked the hills of Galilee together. Now it was time for Him to go. How would He prepare them for what was ahead? What could He say that would leave a deposit of heaven in their very souls?

Perhaps Jesus looked deeply into their expectant eyes, took a deep breath, and then quietly yet firmly said:

Little children, I am still with you a little longer. You will look for Me; and just as I said to the Jews, now I also say to you: "Where I am going, you cannot come." I am giving you a new commandment, that you love one another; just as I have loved you, that you also love one another. By this all people will know that you are My disciples: if you have love for one another.
—John 13:33–35

This is an impossible request made by Jesus to His disciples and therefore to us. We are to love one another as Jesus has loved us. We can't do that in our own strength or through the lens of our culture. The only way we can begin to obey this stirring yet exacting commandment is by asking for the power of the Holy Spirit.

In my own strength, I am unable to love in a fruitful manner even the people I *like* well enough to consider as a friend. I try my best to love the people whom I have chosen as friends and family, but Jesus requires more. He insists that I love people whom I don't like or would prefer not to be in a relationship with. He directs me to love these adversaries of my heart with the all-consuming, non-negotiable, eternal compassion that He has given to me.

> *And He said to him, "'You shall love the Lord your God with all your heart, and with all your soul, and with all your mind.' This is the great and foremost commandment. The second is like it, 'You shall love your neighbor as yourself.'"*
> —Matthew 22:37–39

What does it mean to "love your neighbor as yourself"?

_____

_____

Who is your neighbor?

_____

_____

WHAT LOVE LOOKS LIKE

As you consider what it looks like to love like Jesus loved, perhaps these reminders will help:

+ Love looked like Jesus when He held a child upon His lap.

- Love looked like Jesus when He blessed the woman caught in adultery.
- Love looked like Jesus when He washed the disciples' feet.
- Love looked like Jesus when He told Peter to feed His sheep.
- Love looked like Jesus when He fed hungry people.
- Love looked like Jesus when He called the woman with the issue of blood, "Daughter."
- Love looked like Jesus when He cared about the wedding guests at Cana.
- Love looked like Jesus when He died on the cross.
- Love looked like Jesus.

Love has the hands to caress others without judgment and without reserve. Love has eyes to see someone in pain and to respond to their needs. Love has the ears to hear the silent cries of the destitute and the rejected. Love has feet that run quickly to those in misery. Love has a heart of compassion that gives and gives and gives again.

LIFE QUOTE

No longer can we parse our fellow humans into the categories of "lovable" and "unlovable." If love is an act of the will—not motivated by need, not measuring worth, not requiring reciprocity—then there is no such category as "unlovable."

—Jen Wilkin

VERSE OF THE DAY

But now faith, hope, and love remain, these three; but the greatest of these is love.   —1 Corinthians 13:13

MEANINGFUL MOMENT

Who needs to be touched by the love of Jesus through you today? Listen carefully to the Lord's voice and ask Him to love your world through you.

DAILY DECLARATION

"I declare that I will lay my will down and love like Jesus loved. I will ask the Holy Spirit to give me the strength I need to love those the Lord has placed in my life."

EPILOGUE:
YOU CHOOSE YOUR VERB

What a rich delight it has been to share with you such wonderful ways to truly live—not just exist, but to live abundantly, enthusiastically, and wholeheartedly. I hope you will roll up your sleeves and tackle the business of living a passionate lifestyle with no regrets. Many people walk through life half-awake with no awareness of the beauty of an ordinary day. Don't let that person be you.

Look at the world you have been given with wonder rather than worry; embrace every day with earnest expectation of the Lord's presence and strength. Today is a gift from the Father of creation. Your assignment is to rejoice and be glad in it.

There is no such thing as an *unremarkable day* when you know the Lord. Even routine days present the amazing opportunity to live a life of grand assignment and unusual joy.

How I wish I could infuse my commitment to live without reserve into the veins of your soul. But I can't. I can't live for you, and you can't live for me. Each one of us is responsible for grabbing life with intentional exuberance and creating a masterpiece that will long be remembered.

You choose your own legacy; you choose how you will be remembered.

+ Will you be remembered as angry and bitter?

+ Will your legacy be one of noncommittal malaise?

+ Will you be remembered as enthusiastic and delightful?

+ Will your days be filled with rare gusto and warm fervor?

Look over the verbs presented in this book. Choose five of them to use as your very own.

1. _____

2. _____

3. _____

4. _____

5. _____

THE WHY AND THE HOW

The most exciting and vital day of your life is the day you discover *why* you were born. When you discover your purpose or why God made you, it is a day of unequaled significance. This moment in history would be incomplete without your original fingerprint and unique heartbeat.

Your *why* might include being a teacher, a nurse, or a corporate executive. Your *why* might be fleshed out in the ministry, as an architect, or as a mother.

What is your "why"?

_____

_____

After you discover your why, then you can determine *how* you will accomplish your *why*.

+ Will you encourage others in the business world?

+ Will you give of your wisdom to students?

+ Will you celebrate the delight of an ordinary day with your children?

- Will you walk through the pain of infertility with your patients?

- Will you trust the Lord while you run for public office?

You must select your own set of verbs that will determine your why and your how. Your assignment from heaven is to paint the black and white days of your life with an array of brilliant and defining colors. While you are unable to control most of the circumstances of your life, you are able to decide how you respond to each circumstance. You are the only person alive who can determine what type of life you will live.

Now, make a list of "how" you will live your "why":

1. _____

2. _____

3. _____

Regardless of how horrible or wonderful your past was, it cannot determine your today. Do not give your past that much power.

Regardless of how small it is or how large your income is, it cannot determine the vitality of your life. Don't give money that much power.

Regardless of whether you are single, married, widowed, or divorced, your marital status cannot determine the contentment of your today. Other people don't have that all-consuming power in our lives.

Intentionally live your *why* with an enthusiastic dose of *how* and you just might change the world!

List five verbs perhaps not listed in this book that resonate with the type of life you would love to live:

1. _____

2. _____

3. _____

4. _____

5. _____

FINALLY

What a sweet journey we have been on together! As you live your life in the trenches, I pray you will boldly and joyfully choose to live a life that sparkles with the atmosphere of heaven.

I pray you will outrageously live a life of yielded faith and uncommon belief. I pray you will travel through life with a spring in your step even on the rocky soil of difficult days.

I pray you will discover the peace of a quiet refuge when the storms of life are raging all around you.

I pray you will choose Jesus without reserve. You can trust Him, my friend.

LIFE QUOTE

There is always the danger that we may just do the work for the sake of the work. This is where the respect and the love and the devotion come in—that we do it to God, to Christ, and that's why we try to do it as beautifully as possible.

—Mother Teresa

VERSE OF THE DAY

Whatever you do, do your work heartily, as for the Lord and not for people, knowing that it is from the Lord that you will receive the reward of the inheritance. It is the Lord Christ whom you serve. —Colossians 3:23–24

MEANINGFUL MOMENT

Smile at a stranger. Encourage a family member. Read your Bible. Sing a song. Be generous. Repeat it all tomorrow!

DAILY DECLARATION

"I declare that I was made for today! I will rejoice in the Lord and live a life of enthusiastic engagement!"

ABOUT THE AUTHOR

President and CEO of Carol McLeod Ministries, Carol McLeod is a best-selling author and popular speaker at women's conferences and retreats, where she teaches the Word of God with great joy and enthusiasm. She encourages and empowers women with passionate and practical biblical messages mixed with her own special brand of hope and humor.

Her last two books with Whitaker House received prestigious awards. *At Home in Your Heart* won second place in the 2023 Selah Awards in the devotional category. *Rooms of a Mother's Heart*, a devotional for moms, won the 2022 Director's Choice Award from the Blue Ridge Writers Conference.

Carol's recent titles include *Timeless: The Living and Enduring Word of God*, which dives into the book of 1 Peter, and *Meanwhile: Meeting God in the Wait*, which examines the life of Joseph in Genesis 37–50 and what it means to "wait well" as God labors behind the scenes to work all things together for our good and for His glory.

Her teaching DVD, *The Rooms of a Woman's Heart*, won the Telly Award for excellence in religious programming. Carol's *Significant Women* podcast, which encourages women in every season of life that their story matters, ranks in the top 10 percent of all podcasts internationally.

Carol has also written twenty-five devotionals for YouVersion that have been downloaded nearly four million times around the world. Her weekly blog, *Joy for the Journey*, has been named in the Top 50 Faith Blogs for Women. Carol also writes a monthly devotional for CrossMap.com.

She was the first women's chaplain at Oral Roberts University and received the university's prestigious Alumna of the Year award for "Distinguished Service to God" in 2021.

Carol wed her college sweetheart, Craig, in 1977. She is the mother of five children in heaven and five children on earth. Carol and Craig also happily answer to "Marmee and Pa" for their captivating grandchildren.

Welcome to Our House!

We Have a Special Gift for You

It is our privilege and pleasure to share in your love of Christian books. We are committed to bringing you authors and books that feed, challenge, and enrich your faith.

To show our appreciation, we invite you to sign up to receive a specially selected **Reader Appreciation Gift**, with our compliments. Just go to the Web address at the bottom of this page.

God bless you as you seek a deeper walk with Him!

WE HAVE A GIFT FOR YOU. VISIT:

whpub.me/nonfictionthx

WHITAKER
HOUSE